EARS TO HEAR

EARS TO HEAR

RECOGNIZING AND RESPONDING TO GOD'S CALL

൦൦•൦൦

EDWARD S. LITTLE

MOREHOUSE PUBLISHING
A Continuum imprint
HARRISBURG • LONDON • NEW YORK

Morehouse Publishing
P.O. Box 1321
Harrisburg, Pennsylvania 17105

Morehouse Publishing is an imprint of the
Continuum International publishing group.

Design by Laurie Klein Westhafer

Library of Congress Cataloging-in-Publication Data
Little, Edward S., 1947-
Ears to hear: recognizing and responding to God's call /
Edward S. Little, II.—1st ed.
p. cm.
ISBN 0-8192-1939-8
1. Christian life—Anglican authors. 2. Bible. O.T.—Biography. I.
Title. BV4501.3.L58 2003
248.4—dc21
2002156364

Printed in the United States of America

03   04   05   06   07   6   5   4   3   2   1

CONTENTS

A PERSONAL NOTE

"And when did you receive 'the call'?" people often ask me, with specific intent. When did I come to believe that God had called me to the priesthood? How was I drawn to "professional ministry"? Was it a lifelong yearning or a discovery I made as an adult? The question itself unmasks a problem: that Christians tend to identify "call" with ordination, with seminary training, with full-time, stipendiary service.

The Bible has a different take on the matter. God's people are a called people, and there are no exceptions. "God's gifts and his call are irrevocable" (Rom 11:29). While Paul's reference here is quite narrow—he's talking about God's ongoing care and concern for his chosen people, the Jews—the scriptures teach that God pours out his gifts on every member of the body of Christ (1 Cor 12:7), that God singles out each one of us for eternal fellowship with his Son, Jesus Christ (2 Thess 2:13-14). This book grows out of deep conviction that Christians today need to recover their sense of call.

Ears to Hear: Recognizing and Responding to God's Call is one small part of my response to this divine summons. The people of All Saints Episcopal Church, Bakersfield, California, listened to a series of sermons on God's call that ultimately became the chapters of this book. Together we struggled to understand our own sense of call, and their reflections encouraged and challenged me. All Saints' vestry, at the suggestion of senior warden Bob Hewitt, enabled me to take a sabbatical for sustained writing. I am grateful to them and also to the brothers of Mount Calvary Retreat House (Order of the Holy Cross) and the sisters of St. Mary's Retreat House (Sisters of the Holy Nativity), both in Santa Barbara, California, where most of this book was written. What a joy to be in a place of prayer while I wrestled with sketchy notes and transformed them into prose!

Special thanks are due to a group of nine priests who meet on the first Monday of each month on an avocado ranch in Camarillo, California. Their love and support strengthened me for more than twenty years, from the late 1970s until I moved to the Diocese of Northern Indiana in 2000. Above all, I am grateful to Sylvia, Gregory, and Sharon: My calling as husband and father is a training ground for all the rest. It is there, in my family, that I meet Jesus most profoundly, there that I encounter grace, there that I am loved and sustained.

Many Christians have become sensitized in recent years to the way we use language that refers to human beings and to God. I have sought throughout this book to speak inclusively about people: God's word comes to men and women equally, and God calls us all to a life of discipleship. Language about God presents a more difficult challenge. In the end, I decided to retain a biblical pattern that includes the male pronoun. The alternative, it seems to me, is syntactically awkward and tends to reduce God to a "force." God is neither male nor female, to be sure, and pronouns are at best imprecise; yet those pronouns are scriptural and remind us that God is a person who invites us into relationship. I ask the indulgence of readers for whom this vocabulary is problematic, and I pray the book's overall message will outweigh any barriers of language.

South Bend, Indiana
August 24, 2002
Feast of St. Bartholomew

PROLOGUE

A FOURFOLD CALL TO GOD'S PEOPLE

Revelation 22:17

The invitation was from Her. How did I know? Partly it was the handwriting on the envelope, partly it was intuition. I opened it slowly, almost prayerfully, not wanting to damage either the envelope or its contents. "You Are Invited . . .": me, Ed Little, summoned to my first boy-girl party—by Her. I had been singled out, noticed, addressed, beckoned. Until that moment, I didn't know for sure that She even knew who I was. In class She had never spoken to me, but then, girls would never talk to boys in fifth grade—at least in my day. The invitation from Her was a surprise, an honor, a gift. (Never mind the sad ending to the story: I was so nervous about that boy-girl party that I made myself nauseous and couldn't attend.) But the mere fact that I had been invited changed me. Her glance had come my way. I would never be the same.

Just imagine the transformation when the invitation comes from the living God! There probably won't be as much fanfare—don't count on an envelope in the mail with an unmistakable scrawl—but God's invitation comes to each of us just the same. "Let everyone who is thirsty come. Let anyone who wishes take the water of life as a gift" (Rev 22:17 NRSV). God invites us to quench our thirst, asking only that we drink—that we turn to Jesus, who promises that "those who drink of the water that I will give them will never be thirsty" (John 4:14 NRSV). In the end, this is what God's call is all about: God inviting us back to himself (Matt 11:28), allowing us to partake of his divine life (2 Pet 1:4) and to become agents of his will (2 Cor 5:20). So my working definition of God's call is this: *God's sovereign invitation to individuals and communities in which he bids them to new life and service.*

Two things are presupposed in this definition. First, God is omniscient (Matt 6:8). He knows us better than we know ourselves. He knows our strengths, our weaknesses, our talents, our fears, our joys. Knowing all this and more, he summons us in ways that are perfectly in keeping with who we are. His call is never random. It is always specific and always fitting. Second, we have free will (1 Tim 1:19). God gives us the privilege of accepting or rejecting his call, and he will never force a decision on us; that is how seriously he takes us. And the discovery that the Lord of heaven and earth has singled us out for his call transforms our lives. We can't remain the same under the loving glance of the living God!

God's call, like his gifts, comes in many forms (1 Pet 4:10). At different times we are called in different ways, which means that God's call is not a once-in-a-lifetime event. It is an ongoing process, endlessly varied according to our need and God's purpose.

To what does God call us? *First, God calls us to salvation.* The New Testament says that before Christ entered our lives, we were "dead in [our] transgressions and sins . . . by nature objects of wrath" (Eph 2:1, 3). Something is desperately wrong with us; our built-in self-centeredness separates us from God, from other people, and even from our real selves. God, however, has dramatically intervened in human history through the life, death, and resurrection of his Son, Jesus Christ. He became one of us (John 1:14), died on a cross to secure our forgiveness (Rom 5:8), and rose from the grave to destroy the power of death (Rom 6:8-11). And now Jesus invites us personally to take hold of all that he has done for us. "To all who received [Jesus], to those who believed in his name, he gave the right to become children of God" (John 1:12). We are saved—rescued from sin and death, restored to a relationship with God. And our salvation is by grace: It is a free gift, unearned and unexpected. We appropriate this gift by faith as we entrust our lives to Jesus Christ (Eph 2:8).

Throughout this book we will look at stories of people who have experienced God's call to salvation. The stories are radically different. We will see how some people come to Christ in a sudden flash of light like the apostle Paul (Acts 9:1-9), while others come in a gradual process of growth and insight. The calls are alike only in that the initiative is taken by Jesus, not us. We choose him, but he first chose us (John 15:16; Rom 8:28-30). The apostle Paul, writing years after his conversion, marveled that the risen Christ had singled him out: "Last of all he appeared to me also, as to one abnormally born" (1 Cor 15:8). Salvation is a gift as well as a call. We are the recipients of God's incredible and unmerited love.

Second, God calls us to holiness. Paul begins his first letter to the Corinthians with these words: "Paul, called to be an apostle. ... To the church of God in Corinth, to those sanctified in Christ Jesus and called to be holy" (1 Cor 1:1-2). Paul's letter to the Romans has a similar beginning: "To all in Rome who are loved by God and called to be saints" (Rom 1:7). The words "sanctified," "holy," and "saints" all have the same root in Greek, *hagios*, which means "separated and dedicated." As Christians we have been separated from the world (in the sense that we reject the values of unredeemed culture when they are in conflict with the values of the kingdom of God) and dedicated to God in Christ. We belong to Jesus. On one level, this is a completed process. We are already saints, cleansed and forgiven by the blood of Christ (Heb 9:14) and filled with his Spirit (1 Cor 6:19). Sainthood in the New Testament sense of the word is not earned; it is a status we are given when we open our lives to Jesus Christ. On another level, though, we are not yet fully sanctified (or "sainted"). We have been separated from the world, yet we remain stained. God still has much to do in us. And so Paul can say, "It is God's will that you should be sanctified" (1 Thess 4:3), and then go on with a concrete instance: You must abstain from sexual immorality. Paul ends the discussion by saying, "For God did not call us to be impure, but to live a holy life" (4:7). Holiness, in other words, is a call. Our lives are to be consistent with our status as God's saints.

The New Testament is filled with examples of what holiness looks like. Various lists of the fruit of the Spirit (Rom 5:3-5; Gal 5:22-23; Col 3:12-17; 2 Pet 1:5-7) all point to the way in which the Holy Spirit transforms us from within. Note that the one attribute all the lists have in common is love: the love of Jesus working through us to touch others. Above all, we are to reflect the character of Jesus (2 Cor 3:18) so that when people look at us they catch a glimpse of our Lord himself. "Just as he who called you is holy, so be holy in all you do" (1 Pet 1:15). The process of sanctification is not finished in this life, but in heaven, when we see Jesus face to face, "we shall be like him, for we shall see him as he is" (1 John 3:2). Our call now is to open ourselves to the work of the Spirit. How can I be holy in my workplace? How can I be holy in my neighborhood? How can I be holy in my home, where my spouse and children see me as I really am? Holiness is not a vague, unfocused "goodness." It involves being Jesus' person wherever we are. This is both a call and a challenge.

Third, God calls us to ministry. Sadly, the word "ministry" today has a professional feel—something you do when you've been to seminary and the church has ordained you. But the New Testament has a different perspective. All Christians are ministers—the word simply means "servants"—ordinary Christians as well as people in special leadership positions. Paul writes, "The gifts [Christ] gave were that some would be apostles, some prophets, some evangelists, some pastors and teachers" (Eph 4:11 NRSV). He is here describing leaders in the Christian community. And what is the purpose of the leaders' ministry? "To equip the saints for the work of ministry" (4:12 NRSV); to enable each member of the body of Christ to discover and carry out the Lord's call. Ministry is both general and specific. In a general sense, we are all called to service; but we are called to specific tasks within that general summons. Thus Jesus called James and John, among others, to be numbered among the Twelve (Matt 4:21). Thus Paul was called to be an apostle (1 Cor 1:1; Gal 1:15; et al.). Thus Paul and Barnabas were called to carry the gospel into the Mediterranean basin (Acts 13:2). Thus the Jews were set apart as God's chosen people and given an irrevocable call (Rom 11:29). "We are God's workmanship, created in Christ Jesus to do good works, which God prepared in advance for us to do" (Eph 2:10). From all eternity, God has planned for our ministry.

In Chapter 4 we will look at the story of Bezalel and Oholiab, craftsmen who were called to build a portable worship center called the tabernacle. Their ministry consisted of recognizing their gifts and talents and putting them at the Lord's disposal. Our ministry may be a showy and public one, known in the church and beyond, or it may be quiet and unnoticed. We need to see our ministry as broadly as possible, not limiting it to the church or to specifically "religious" activities. Our call may well send us out into the world, into a place of darkness, where we can shine with the light of Christ.

Fourth, God calls us to community. Belonging to Jesus and belonging to his people are inextricably linked in the New Testament. And so in one place Paul can say, "All of you who were baptized into Christ have clothed yourselves with Christ" (Gal 3:27); and in another, "We were all baptized by one Spirit into one body [that is, the Church]" (1 Cor 12:13). Paul is neither contradicting himself nor confused in his baptismal theology. Both statements are true: Baptism is the sign of belonging to Jesus Christ and to his body, the Church. There is no specific statement in the New Testament joining "call" to "community," yet the word "church" itself is filled with a meaning not conveyed in our English translations. The Greek word usually translated "church" is *ekklesia,* a compound that means the "called-out ones." Every mention of "the church" reminds us of our call to community.

There are two levels to this call. Paul talks about "the church" (Col 1:18) and "the churches" (2 Cor 11:28), by which he is referring first to the worldwide body of which Jesus is the head and second to the specific, local manifestation of this body. We are called to both. In baptism we join that organism that's found on every continent in virtually every nation in the world, multicultural, multiracial, more than one billion in number: the Church. At the same time, God calls us to belong to a church, to an expression of the worldwide Church in our own locale. When Christians move to a new city and start "looking for a church," they are doing more than mere comparison shopping. Although they may not know the vocabulary, they are answering God's call to community.

God's call comes to us in many ways. Sometimes it involves a theophany—a dramatic manifestation of the presence of God, as Moses and Isaiah experienced. Sometimes it comes in an audible voice, as it did for Abraham, Gideon, Jeremiah, and Jacob. Sometimes we simply experience an inner prompting, a "sound of sheer silence" (1 Kgs 19:12 NRSV), quiet and inaudible, just as Elijah did. Sometimes God's call comes through another person, as it did for Elisha, David, Bezalel, Oholiab, and Zerubbabel. Sometimes someone else simply helps us to listen for God's voice in the same way that someone did for Samuel and Deborah. Sometimes the call comes when we are broken (Hosea) or busy (Amos). Sometimes God's call forces us to face our worst fears (Joshua) or simply asks a question (Esther). There is no "right" way to hear God. His call comes in a multitude of wrappings, and part of our task as Christians is to discern his voice in the midst of our day-to-day lives. It comes at surprising times, in surprising places, through surprising people.

We begin our journey into God's call at the end of the

biblical drama, in the new Jerusalem, where Jesus invites us to drink. "Let everyone who is thirsty come. Let anyone who wishes take the water of life as a gift" (Rev 22:17 NRSV). The call of Jesus Christ is the call of One who extends his hand in love, drawing us to himself, transforming our lives, sending us out in his name, giving us brothers and sisters to travel with us on our journey.

Questions for Discussion

1. How did Jesus Christ first become a living reality for you?

2. What kind of mental images does the word "holiness" bring to mind? Are they positive or negative? What would "holy living" mean in your life today?

3. Which areas of your life can you identify as "ministries"? Do you sense an inner disquiet that may indicate a call to new ministry?

4. What are the communities to which you belong? How did they enter your life, and you theirs?

-1-

CALLED TO INSECURITY: ABRAHAM

Genesis 11:31-12:4

"God told us to move to northern California," Tom said.

I looked at Tom and Eileen across my desk and wondered if he were joking. Tom's face was serious enough, but I couldn't imagine that he meant what he had just told me.

"Really, now. What did you come to see me about?"

"I mean it," Tom said. "Eileen and I both feel that the Lord wants us to sell our house and move to northern California."

"But what are you going to do there?" I asked. "Where will you live? How will you support yourselves and your children?"

"I don't know. God hasn't told us yet."

I knew Tom and Eileen as steady, committed Christians. Tom was a successful attorney, and Eileen had a satisfying job with an advertising agency. Their marriage was the second for both; between them they had five teenagers, all living at home with them. Their two incomes barely covered the cost of feeding and clothing their children and making an enormous house payment. They had arrived in the parish about the same time that I did, five years before, and we had quickly become friends. Tom and Eileen were biblically literate, articulate about their faith, willing to take risks for the Lord. But was God asking them to do *this?*

Several months later, I stood with them in front of their house, watching the last of their possessions being loaded into the moving van. Everything was to be put in storage. They had sold their home, put the equity in the bank to cover living expenses, and filled two cars with suitcases. Now they were preparing to drive . . . where? They didn't know. They believed, somehow, that the Lord was leading them north, to an indefinite location, with an indefinite plan. As they prayed separately and together, Tom and Eileen had come to the same conclusion: God wanted them to leave everything behind and go north, where, they believed, God would show them what they were to do.

Why would two otherwise sane Christians do such an insane thing? I was far from convinced that they had really heard a call from the Lord. Still, I stood and prayed with them that the Lord would accomplish his purpose, whatever that was. They squeezed into their cars, Tom and Eileen and the teenagers, and drove away.

Their move prompted me to ask myself a question. Does God challenge people to take risks? Does he ask people to leave behind everything safe and secure and to follow blindly without a hint of a destination? Most Christians would agree that Jesus calls us to "step out in faith," but when it comes to specifics—to the daily business of making a living, supporting a family, getting through school—we shrink back. What does God really require? Consider our father in the faith, Abraham.

> Terah took his son Abram, his grandson Lot son of Haran, and his daughter-in-law Sarai, the wife of his son Abram, and together they set out from Ur of the Chaldeans to go to Canaan. But when they came to Haran, they settled there. Terah lived 205 years, and he died in Haran. (Gen 11:31-32)

Abraham probably heard God's call when he lived in Ur, a city on the Euphrates River in southern Mesopotamia. In its day, two thousand years or so before the birth of Jesus, Ur was a center of trade and learning. It had a harbor, commercial buildings, and running water. There were two-story homes with courtyards and a sanitary system. Its library contained a vast number of clay books covering a variety of subjects, from religion to mathematics to grammar. Magnificent temples and private chapels honored a pantheon of gods and goddesses, among whose worshipers was Abraham's family (Josh 24:2).

Ur was, in other words, a wonderful place to live. Nomads from the desert would envy anyone who had the privilege of residing in this complex and wealthy city. Thus God's call to Abraham must have been shocking and unimaginable:

> The LORD had said to Abram, "Leave your country, your people and your father's household and go to the land I will show you.
>
> "I will make you into a great nation
> and I will bless you;
> I will make your name great,
> and you will be a blessing.
> I will bless those who bless you,
> and whoever curses you I will curse;
> and all peoples on earth
> will be blessed through you."
> (Gen 12:1-3)

Soon after Abraham received God's call, his father, Terah, moved the family to Haran in northwest Mesopotamia—not Ur, certainly, but at least it was within Ur's cultural orbit. In time, though, Abraham remembered God's words to him. "The LORD had said to Abram, 'Leave your country. . . .'" Finally, he complied. "So Abram left, as the LORD had told him; and Lot went with him. Abram was seventy-five years old when he set out from Haran" (Gen 12:4).

God's call to Abraham contains a double command and a double promise. The first command is "Leave." Leave the familiar—the landscapes you've looked at for years, the culture that's nourished you. Leave behind *everything*: amenities, language, religion, even family. God was asking Abraham for a radical act of obedience. This was to be no short-term mission, no quick trip to a foreign country and back. God was commanding permanent separation from everything Abraham knew.

To this, God added a second command: "Go." Step out and follow my lead, though you don't know where it will take you. I have a place for you, God was saying, but you won't know it until you get there. This second command would eventually become a gift; God promised Abraham that the land to which he was sent would someday belong to his offspring, though now it was occupied by strangers (Gen 13:14-15; 17:8).

Abraham was a prime candidate for culture shock. God took him away from the civilization that had given him birth, from a culture that was sophisticated and advanced, and sent him to a place where he would be a foreigner. No one would know him, no one would speak his language, no one would share his cultural assumptions. Everything would be different, from the mode of transportation to the medium of exchange.

God's double promise to the childless, seventy-five-year-old Abraham first involved descendants: "I will make you into a great nation." Later God would reiterate and dramatize his promise: "'Look up at the heavens and count the stars—if indeed you can count them.' Then [the LORD] said to him, 'So shall your offspring be'" (Gen 15:5; see also 13:14-16; 17:15-16; 22:17). With these extraordinary promises, the Lord was not simply setting apart an individual. He was creating a *people* to be his own.

In the second part of his promise, God pledged blessing to and through Abraham. You will be blessed, God told him, and so will those who look upon you favorably. Some day, in fact, the whole family of nations on earth will be blessed with the blessing that you will receive. It is through you and your descendants, God said, that the whole earth will be blessed. Abraham could not have understood the implications of these promises. But though he didn't understand, he obeyed.

God called Abraham to move from security to insecurity, from the known to the unknown, from the predictable to the unpredictable, singling him out to be the model of obedient and costly faith. The old gods of Ur may have been comfortably reliable, easily placated. But the God who called Abraham was a God who loved and a God who demanded. Two thousand years later, the writer of the Letter to the Hebrews summed up God's call and Abraham's response: "By faith Abraham, when called to go to a place he would later receive as his inheritance, obeyed and went, even though he did not know where he was going. By faith he made his home in the promised land like a stranger in a foreign country" (Heb 11:8-9).

God commanded Abraham to risk. He could do that because he himself is a risk-taker. The story of the Bible, after all, is the story of God taking risks, from start to finish. "In the beginning God created the heavens and the earth" (Gen 1:1). The very act of creation involved risk, as God called into being a reality separate from himself, created and dependent, infused with his life and yet not divine. Even more risky, God created the human race. "Then God said, 'Let us make humankind in our image, according to our likeness; and let them have dominion'" over the natural order (Gen 1:26 NRSV). God endowed his creatures with that dangerous quality, free will, and thus gave them the option to reject him. God's risk set in motion a chain of events that would move from the Garden of Eden to the Garden of Gethsemane to the cross and the empty tomb.

But there's more. Having been rejected by his creatures, God continued to risk. He chose a particular nation of people to be his light-bearers in a dark world. "Now if you obey me fully and keep my covenant, then out of all nations you will be my treasured possession . . . a kingdom of priests and a holy nation" (Ex 19:5-6). The risk is unmasked in that terrible word "if." God acknowledged, even as he called his people, that they might well reject him as surely as their forebears had done in the Garden.

And in fact they did so, over and over. Much of the story of the Old Testament is the story of God seeking his people even as they refuse to be sought. "'Return, faithless Israel,' declares the LORD, 'I will frown on you no longer, for I am merciful,' declares the LORD" (Jer 3:12). Yet God's people turned their backs on their King and declined his offer of love and forgiveness.

In the New Testament, God took the ultimate risk. He entered personally into the insecurity of our world, the world of time and space, of form and matter. He was born, and lived, and died, and rose again. "In the beginning was the Word, and the Word was with God, and the Word was God. . . . The Word became flesh and made his dwelling among us" (John 1:1, 14). In entering our world, God experienced how tenuous human life is, how frail, how easily broken. God in Jesus Christ put aside the prerogatives of deity to risk everything for us. "Being in very nature God, [Jesus] did not consider equality with God something to be grasped, but made himself nothing, taking the very nature of a servant, being made in human likeness. And being found in appearance as a man, he humbled himself and became obedient to death—even death on a cross!" (Phil 2:6-8). Yes, in the end Jesus rose from the dead, and "God exalted him to the highest place and gave him the name that is above every name, that at the name of Jesus every knee should bow" (2:9-10). But Jesus' exaltation was possible only because he had entered the insecurity of our world and suffered the loss of everything. Risk is at the heart of God's dealings with us.

The Bible is the story not only of God's risks but of the risks God asks people to take. "As Jesus passed along the Sea of Galilee, he saw Simon and his brother Andrew casting a net into the sea—for they were fishermen. And Jesus said to them, 'Follow me and I will make you fish for people.' And immediately they left their nets and followed him" (Mark 1:16-18 NRSV). Jesus called them to abandon their livelihood and their security, risking everything for him. The New Testament is filled with story after story of persons challenged to abandon the familiar for the sake of an unknown future with Jesus. Matthew the tax collector, Nathanael the skeptic, and Saul the Pharisee all heard Jesus' invitation: "Follow me."

All of this leads me to ask two questions. The first is this: *What is your Ur?* What is your place of security and familiarity? It may be your physical environment—the house where you live; the town you grew up in; the suburb with its collection of shopping centers, parks, and neighborhoods. It may be a job that doesn't challenge you—but doesn't stress you, either, or a church that seems to ask little more than Sunday attendance and money in the plate. "Ur" can be your family, your finances, or the way you live your daily life. Our early-twenty-first-century culture, with its instant communication links, its omnipresent television screen, its ease of transportation, can also represent "Ur." Are there ways your environment has become so comfortable that you wouldn't change it, even for Jesus' sake?

There's a spiritual component to "Ur" as well, referring not so much to external environment as to the climate of the heart. This may include values and attitudes that, perhaps unconsciously, we imbibe from our culture. It's a culture that exalts the individual almost to the point of narcissism, a culture that takes for its motto "Grab for all the gusto you can!" We can't help but be transformed by hours of television viewing or web surfing— even a cursory flip through the dozens (or hundreds) of channels on the cable box provides glimpses of almost casually presented greed and disrespect, murder and fornication. On a conscious level, we may reject these values; but without knowing that it's happening, we can soak them in. They become another component of our "Ur."

Our spiritual life also can become so comfortable that it doesn't stretch us into deeper commitment to Jesus Christ—we can be in the midst of "Ur" even as we pray! Our relationship with the Lord can get stagnant, conventional, as we find ourselves no longer growing, no longer listening for the Lord's voice, no longer yearning to read and reflect on the Scriptures. Our love for Jesus becomes, in Jesus' words to the Laodiceans, "lukewarm—neither hot nor cold" (Rev 3:16). We may know intuitively that something is wrong but have no desire to change. Our discipleship has become comfortable: It has become our "Ur."

Second, *What is the promised land to which God calls you?* What "new thing" is God presenting to you (see Isa 43:19)? It may not be as dramatic as Abraham's journey from Ur to the promised land or as risky as Tom and Eileen's move across the state of California. God's call may be external, affecting your job, your time, the way you spend your money, the quality of your relationships with family or friends, where you live and how you live. So ask yourself: How does Jesus want me to serve him today, in the world and in the church? In what specific ways does he call me to share the Good News with a world so hungry that it no longer recognizes the hunger pains?

Of course, some calls are not to ministry but are more inward—perhaps a challenge to your prayer life or your willingness to risk encounter with the living God. Nothing is exempt from God's call. "Leave" and "Go" are essential components of the way God deals with us. The particulars vary from person to person because God has created and calls each of us uniquely.

In calling Abraham, God had a special word about his relationship with him. "But you, O Israel, my servant, Jacob, whom I have chosen, you descendants of *Abraham my friend . . .*" (Isa 41:8, italics mine; see also 2 Chr 20:7; Jas 2:23). Jesus spoke the same word to his disciples. "You are my friends if you do what I command. I no longer call you servants, because a servant does not know his master's business. Instead, I have called you friends" (John 15:14-15). The word "friend" represents the heart of God, God's longing for us. He wants us to know the joy of companionship with his Son, Jesus, and we can find it in our openness to his call. As we say yes to his command to leave and go, as we move away from the security of "Ur" into the insecurity of obedience, we discover the faithfulness of God and a depth of friendship beyond our imagining.

Tom and Eileen made this discovery. Their journey took them to a small town in northern California where, months later, they started a safe house for abused women and children. For years they brought the love and compassion of Jesus to people who had been bruised by life. When they left Orange County in the Los Angeles basin, they had no idea what God had in mind, but in obeying, they discovered his purpose. Most of us may never receive a call as dramatic and demanding as Abraham's or Tom and Eileen's. I never have. Even my moves from place to place in the course of three decades of ministry have been unspectacular, wrenching only in my heart. But however the Lord calls—quietly so that only we can hear, or loudly in a way that transfigures the outer shape of our lives—God's call is meant to lead us fully into his friendship.

Questions for Discussion

1. Where do you feel most comfortable, settled, and at home? Why?

2. How in the past have you perceived that it was time to "move on," physically or spiritually? Are there ways that you sense God might be asking you to "move on" today? What are the road-blocks to such a move—in your circumstances, or in your heart?

3. Abraham's call to leave Ur and travel to an unspecified destination involved moving from the familiar to the unknown. Do you believe God has ever asked you to make such a move?

4. "Risk" is a two-edged sword: It can bring excitement, challenge, renewed vision; it can also bring fear, doubt, and even despair. How do you react to the possibility of risk in God's call to you?

-2-

GOD'S PERSISTENT CALL: JACOB

Genesis 28:10-22; 32:22-32

Penuel's conversion was an accident. Or so it seemed.

In the spring of 1990 I traveled to Uganda to lead a series of conferences for Christian leaders and spent one Sunday morning preaching at St. Francis Chapel, the Anglican chapel of Makerere University in Kampala. The final service of the day, in a language called Lugbara, required me to speak through an interpreter. I stood in the center of the chancel, a young man named Penuel at my right, and after each ten- or fifteen-second burst in English, Penuel translated my words into Lugbara. I spoke on John 7:37-39 and Jesus' promise that the Holy Spirit will flow through believers as a river of life-giving water. By the sermon's end, Penuel and I had fallen into a comfortable rhythm— English, Lugbara, English, Lugbara.

I forgot all about this partnership until, months later, I received a letter from the chaplain at St. Francis. "I thought you would like to know," Ben wrote, "that the after-effects of your visit are being felt. Sunday 22 July, a youth by the name of Penuel came to the vestry looking very confused. On being asked, he told me that ever since he interpreted for you . . . he has remained with a challenge. He said that as you preached and he interpreted for you, he felt that you were saying the things you believed while he was saying the things he never believed. . . . On 22 July instead of going to the Lugbara service he came to me and I had the chance of being his midwife as he was born into the new family—God's family. It sure took a long time to sink in but it did: Praise the Lord."

But Penuel's conversion was no accident. In a patchwork of

languages, God had called Penuel—English, Lugbara, whatever it took, God sent the word out loud and clear. As I read Ben's letter and pondered Penuel's conversion, I thought of Francis Thompson's poem "The Hound of Heaven," which pictures Jesus as a dog relentlessly pursuing its prey.

> I fled Him, down the nights and down the days;
> I fled Him, down the arches of the years;
> I fled Him, down the labyrinthine ways
> Of my own mind; and in the mist of tears
> I hid from Him, and under running laughter.
> Up vistaed hopes I sped;
> And shot, precipitated,
> Adown Titanic glooms of chasmed fears,
> From those strong Feet that followed, followed after.
> But with unhurrying chase,
> And unperturbèd pace,
> Deliberate speed, majestic instancy,
> They beat—and a Voice beat
> More instant than the Feet—
> "All things betray thee, who betrayest Me."[1]

The strong Feet, the insistent Voice—the Hound of Heaven is persistent. He will never let us go, will never stop pursuing us and drawing us to himself, will never cease to call. We may refuse to hear; we may reject his call. But he will not reject us. He will follow us relentlessly, like the Hound, just as he followed Penuel and one of the Bible's most unpleasant characters—the patriarch Jacob.

Abraham and Sarah finally had a son, Isaac (Gen 21:1-3), who in turn married Rebekah (24:66-67). Isaac and Rebekah produced two sons, a set of twins. Even the circumstances of their birth tell us that problems would inevitably follow. Esau was born first. His name means "hairy," and hairy he was. Jacob followed, grasping Esau's heel. His name is descriptive too. It means "He grasps the heel," though it might be more to the point simply to call him "The Grabber" (25:24-26). His character became evident early in life. He was selfish, greedy, dishonest; it is hard to find a less sympathetic personality in the entire Bible.

Two early incidents illustrate Jacob's character. In the first, Esau returned home from a long day of hunting, famished and ready for a meal. Jacob, an indoors kind of person, happened to be cooking some stew. But Jacob refused to allow his brother to eat until Esau agreed to sell him his birthright—including his inheritance rights as the firstborn son. Jacob took advantage of Esau's hunger—and his shortsightedness—to cheat him out of what should have been his (25:27-34).

In the second incident, Jacob cheated his brother even more deliberately. Encouraged by his mother, Jacob posed as Esau, wearing the older brother's clothes and covering his hands and neck with goatskin to simulate Esau's hairiness. Then he brought the blind Isaac some food. "Ah, the smell of my son is like the smell of a field that the LORD has blessed" (Gen 27:27), Isaac said, and he conferred on Jacob a blessing that should have been reserved for the firstborn: "May nations serve you and peoples bow down to you. Be lord over your brothers" (27:29). When Esau heard about this, he was understandably furious. "The days of mourning for my father are near" he said. "Then I will kill my brother Jacob" (27:41). The Grabber's greed shattered his home.

After Esau's threat, Jacob fled, but God persistently called him back. Each call came in the midst of crisis. When Jacob left home, for example, he camped at a place that would later be called Bethel. There he "had a dream in which he saw a stairway resting on the earth, with its top reaching to heaven, and the angels of God were ascending and descending on it" (28:12). God did three things. First, he identified himself: "I am the LORD, the God of your father Abraham and the God of Isaac" (28:13).

Second, he reiterated the promises that he had made earlier to Abraham and Isaac, promises of land, offspring, and measureless blessing. Third, he told Jacob, "I will not leave you until I have done what I have promised you" (28:15). Jacob reacted piously. "Surely the LORD is in this place, and I was not aware of it. . . . How awesome is this place! This is none other than the house of God; this is the gate of heaven" (28:16-17). Then he vowed, "If God will be with me and will watch over me on this journey I am taking . . . , then the LORD will be my God and this stone that I have set up as a pillar will be God's house, and of all that you give me I will give you a tenth" (28:20-23).

It would be wonderful if we could see an immediate change in Jacob's character following his first call. But nothing of the sort happened. Jacob came to Paddan Aram, where he met and married Rachel and Leah, daughters of his Uncle Laban. And eventually Jacob's natural instincts took over again: He cheated his father-in-law out of a substantial number of sheep and left town without even saying good-bye. Laban gave chase, and he and Jacob finally came to an uneasy truce in Gilead. Jacob continued on his way, sending word ahead to Esau of his imminent arrival (29:1-32:6).

As he prepared to meet Esau, Jacob camped alone on the far bank of the Jabbok River, and it was there that God called him again, even more dramatically than at Bethel.

> A man wrestled with him till daybreak. When the man saw that he could not overpower him, he touched the socket of Jacob's hip so that his hip was wrenched as he wrestled with the man. Then the man said, "Let me go, for it is daybreak."
> But Jacob replied, "I will not let you go unless you bless me."
> The man asked him, "What is your name?"
> "Jacob," he answered.

Then the man said, "Your name will no longer be
Jacob, but Israel [which means "he struggles with
God"], because you have struggled with God and with
men and have overcome."
Jacob said, "Please tell me your name."
But he replied, "Why do you ask my name?" Then he
blessed him there. (32:24-29)

Who was the man? God? An angelic being? It's not really clear.
But what *is* clear is that Jacob was again involved in a divine-
human encounter, and his new name symbolized the new call
that God intended for him.

The story of Jacob tells the story of God's relentless love.
What can we learn from Jacob's experience?

First, our God is a persistent God. Jacob showed so little
promise for so long that a God in our image would have given up
early in the story. But God is not in our image—and we can be
grateful for that! He sees not only what is but what can be. He
sees as reality what is yet only potential, and then calls it forth.
Thus with Jacob. Yes, God saw The Grabber—grasping, self-
serving, duplicitous. "O God, you know my foolishness, and my
faults are not hidden from you" (Ps 69:6 BCP)—this prayer
could have been prayed by Jacob himself. God knew Jacob's sin
better than Jacob did, but God also saw The God-Struggler, the
one who wrestled with the Lord and, in time, was transformed
by the encounter. More than that, God called The God-Struggler
forth from the unlikely source of The Grabber—called strength
forth from moral weakness, obedience from rebellion. God's
persistence won in the end. God never let Jacob go, though he
fought and ran and hid.

God's relentless pursuit is a consistent biblical pattern.
Look, for example, at the story of Saul the Pharisee. Saul's
conversion seems, at first glance, a sudden thing—on the way to
Damascus—a flashing light and a thundering voice: "Saul, Saul,

why do you persecute me?" . . . "Who are you, Lord?" Saul asked. "I am Jesus, whom you are persecuting" (Acts 9:4-5). Saul was undone, captured by the one he had tried to destroy. Later, on reflection, Saul (who had now become the Apostle Paul) saw a broader picture and realized the Lord had actually been pursuing him *since birth*: "God . . . set me apart before I was born and called me through his grace" (Gal 1:15 NRSV).

Donald Coggan, late Archbishop of Canterbury, reminds us that "Saul was there" at the stoning of Stephen, "giving approval to his death" (Acts 8:1). Saul had heard Stephen commend his spirit to Jesus and then pray for his persecutors (7:59-60). Coggan writes, "We think of the conversion of St. Paul as being a sudden one. Indeed, it is often taken as the classic example of such conversions. But this is only very partially true. Adolf Deissmann pointed out that there was much inflammable material on which the lightning of Damascus was to strike. Stephen provided much of that material. . . . The face of Stephen—how could he ever forget it? The voice of Stephen, calling on the Lord to receive his spirit and forgive his murderers, rang in his ears sleepless night after sleepless night, until at last he capitulated to the love of God in Christ."[2] The persistence of God called forth Paul from Saul.

Christians often talk about God as a "personal" God and a relationship with Jesus Christ as a "personal" one. If we use "personal" to mean exclusive and private (as though to imply, "He's *my* Lord, not yours!"), the word is not appropriate. On the other hand, if we use "personal" to say something about God's character, it is very much to the point. In the eighteenth century, Deists believed in a Creator God who made the universe at the beginning of time, set natural laws in motion as a watchmaker winds a clock, and then withdrew to allow creation to work itself out. But Christians have a very different view. God is *personal.* He continues to involve himself in his creation, interact with his creatures, and call his people to faith and obedience. He will never stop doing so. He is persistent.

We can experience God's persistence in any number of ways. It can come in the form of conscience, when we have the sense that our actions don't line up with what we know to be right and true. It can come as a vague dissatisfaction, when we feel that life isn't what it should be and that something—or Someone—is missing. It can come as we pray, as we read the Bible and let its message soak in, as we worship God in the Christian community. Each of us is unique to the Lord, and each of us will experience God's persistent call differently.

Second, God will not force us to comply with his call. Had I been the Creator rather than God, I perhaps would have made a substantially different universe. One thing would certainly be changed: the messy business of the free will of humankind. Free will leads to all sorts of problems: sin, rebellion, moral chaos. Had men and women been "programmed" to obey God from the start, our planet would be a much neater place. No one would make wrong choices. No one would say no. God, however, has chosen a different way. He has created us to make decisions. The story of the rich young man (Mark 10:17-23) reminds us that Jesus honors our freedom so completely that he gives us the freedom to turn away from him.

At the age of 14, I began to search for the meaning of life. As part of my exploration, I would tune in to Billy Graham on the radio every Sunday night about 9:00 P.M. for the *Hour of Decision*. I would lay on my bed in the darkness and listen to the Good News, week after week. Finally, one night Billy Graham extended an invitation in words like these: "If you're in bed with the lights out listening to me on the radio, I want you to do something right now." He certainly had my attention! "I want you to draw an imaginary circle on your floor, kneel down in the center of the circle, and pray a prayer inviting Jesus into your life as Lord and Savior. I ask you to do it *right now*." In the stillness of my bedroom I asked myself: *Do I really want to do this? Do*

I want to allow Jesus to come in and disrupt my life? After a long pause, I answered: *No.* I refused the offer. It was another five years before I prayed the prayer that Billy Graham had urged me to pray.

Third, God gives us joy as we obey his persistent call. Just look at Jacob. By the time we read about him again, in Genesis 49, he's a transformed man—not perfect, certainly, but wise, discerning, even gentle. Something has happened to him. He has submitted himself to the Lord and his call and has finally come to a measure of peace, with his family and with God. "When Jacob had finished giving instructions to his sons, he drew his feet up into the bed, breathed his last and was gathered to his people" (Gen 49:33). What a change from The Grabber who had lied to his father, cheated his brother, swindled his father-in-law, and fled in terror!

A few years ago, driving into Manhattan on I-95, I took a wrong turn onto the Henry Hudson Parkway and ended up, quite by accident, in Washington Heights, on the northern tip of the island, looking across at the George Washington Bridge and the New Jersey Palisades. The jumble of vehicles and people disoriented me. Cars honked, pedestrians shouted, and I wasn't sure where to go or how to get there. Although I'm a New York native, I hadn't lived in the city since my teens, and I'd rarely driven in Manhattan. In desperation I headed south, toward Midtown, and as I pulled up at a stoplight I looked out the car window—and saw the Episcopal Church of the Holy Rood. Then I remembered. When I was an infant, my parents had lived in Washington Heights, and I had been baptized at Holy Rood. Now, five decades later, I gazed at the place where my Christian life began and was overwhelmed by the wonder of God's persistent love. Through all of my yes's and no's, God had relentlessly drawn me to himself—through failures and successes, through inarticulate yearnings, through people, and through silence. Before I knew him, he knew and loved me.

Jacob's story invites us to ponder God's persistence and our response. How has Jesus knocked on the door of our hearts (Rev 3:20), not once but over and over? Who are the persons and what are the events that have drawn us more deeply into a relationship with the Lord of the universe? How have we obeyed? How have we refused? Jacob's story adds one more piece of good news— that when we refuse, God is not done with us. "His love endures forever" (Ps 136:1).

Questions for Discussion

1.   What strategies have you developed to escape God's call?

2.   How has God pursued you as you evaded his call? Who were the people and what were the events that signaled the approach of the Hound of Heaven?

3.   God changed Jacob's name to Israel: The Grabber became The God-Struggler. God saw hidden strengths in this man, hidden even from Jacob himself. Can you think of a time when discovering something about yourself has led you to understand more clearly God's call on your life?

4.   What are the persistent yearnings in your life? How do they point you to a divine summons?

---

[1] Francis Thompson, *The Hound of Heaven* (Harrisburg, PA: Morehouse, 1996).

[2] Donald Coggan, *The Prayers of the New Testament* (New York: Harper and Row, 1967), 80–81.

-3-

OBJECTIONS TO GOD'S CALL: MOSES

Exodus 3:1-4:17

When the phone rings at 2:00 A.M., my first thought is, *Who died?* So it was that morning when I was jarred into consciousness by an insistent ring, the harbinger, I assumed, of a deathbed summons. The familiar voice on the other end of the line, however, sounded far away. "Oh, Father Ed, I'm sorry to wake you up so early, but I just don't know what to do." It was a parishioner named Andrea. "I'm here in Maryland visiting my aunt, and she's been taken to the hospital, some sort of heart attack, and the doctors say she probably won't make it, and I don't know who to call. I don't know anybody here." Words came tumbling out, and I tried to untangle them in my early-morning mental fog. "You see, Aunt Harriet has never gone to church, and she doesn't much believe in anything, and now here she is, hooked up to tubes. She can't even speak, there's a respirator down her throat, and she might die, and what am I supposed to say to her?"

Tell her about Jesus, I said. Tell her that Jesus loves her. Tell her that Jesus is right there in that intensive care unit. "Oh, but, Father Ed, can't you see? I'm not trained to do this! I mean, you're a priest and all, and you've been to seminary, and you've got the right words. I don't have the words. I'm just a regular person!" It's not hard, I told Andrea. You don't need to be a theologian. Say what's in your heart, and the Holy Spirit will take care of the rest. "But, Father Ed," she insisted, "you don't understand. I've never done anything like this before. I just can't!"

"I just can't!"—familiar words. Throughout salvation history, many of God's people have responded to his call with the same refrain: "I just can't." Though he went on to become one of the Bible's most notable leaders, Moses, like Andrea, also responded to God's call with great reluctance.

The circumstances leading to Moses' call actually began several centuries earlier. The family of Jacob had migrated to Egypt and grown, and grown, and grown, to the point that God's promise to Abraham that his descendants would be "as numerous as the stars in the sky and as the sand on the seashore" (Gen 22:17) began to be fulfilled. But the Book of Exodus opens ominously: "Then a new king, who did not know about Joseph [Jacob's son], came to power in Egypt" (1:8). Ultimately, God's people were converted into slave laborers, with increasingly harsh burdens. At one point, Pharaoh became so threatened by the Hebrews' astonishing population increase that he ordered the extermination of all male babies. (Genocide is no new phenomenon for the Jews.) Moses, however, was miraculously preserved. His mother placed him in a papyrus basket and put it in the Nile; Pharaoh's daughter found him and "he became her son" (2:10). Moses the Hebrew was raised in the royal household of Egypt. Later, Moses, intervening in a dispute between a Hebrew and an Egyptian, killed the Egyptian. "When Pharaoh heard of this, he tried to kill Moses, but Moses fled from Pharaoh" into the Sinai peninsula (2:15). There he married and settled into life as a shepherd.

Decades passed. One day Moses was tending his father-in-law's flock near the base of Mount Sinai, and God called him. "The angel of the LORD appeared to him in flames of fire from within a bush. Moses saw that though the bush was on fire it did not burn up. . . . God called to him from within the bush, 'Moses! Moses!' And Moses said, 'Here I am'" (3:2, 4). God ordered Moses to remove his sandals—a sign that Moses was standing on holy ground—and identified himself as the God of Abraham, Isaac, and Jacob. "At this, Moses hid his face, because he was afraid to look at God" (3:6). Then God issued his call to Moses. "The LORD said, 'I have indeed seen the misery of my people in Egypt. I have heard them crying out because of their slave drivers, and I am concerned about their suffering. So I have come down to rescue them from the hand of the Egyptians. . . . So now, go. I am sending you to Pharaoh to bring my people the Israelites out of Egypt'" (3:7-8, 10).

I wish I could say that Moses accepted God's call and immediately traveled to Egypt, but that didn't happen. Moses' answer to God's call was a resounding "NO!" In fact, he raised five objections to God's call. Let's look at each—and at God's response—and see how we sometimes raise the same objections.

The first objection involved Moses' *qualifications*. "Moses said to God, 'Who am I, that I should go to Pharaoh and bring the Israelites out of Egypt?'" (3:11). What was Moses saying? He was claiming, in effect, that he was not important enough for the job—he didn't have the "pull" or the stature to face down the most powerful monarch in the world. After all, why should Pharaoh listen to a renegade foster-brother-turned-shepherd? There must be someone else more qualified for the job—someone with the personal charisma, the strength of character, and the commitment to God that would enable him to take on Pharaoh.

As I write these words, I hear myself saying—and perhaps you hear yourself too—"Who am I?" Who am I—to claim to be a channel of God's love to others? Who am I—to share my faith in Jesus Christ? Who am I—to pray for the sick, to comfort the grieving, to speak out against injustice, even to claim to be raising children in the knowledge and love of the Lord? There must be someone else more qualified, someone else who could do it better.

Similarly, Christians often imagine something of a "qualification gap" between clergy and laity, an unbiblical division in the Body of Christ. Yes, there is a role assigned to Christian leaders, as we saw in the Prologue: "to equip the saints for the work of ministry" (Eph 4:12 NRSV), to train and encourage and guide God's people to exercise their giftedness in response to their own call in the Church and in the world. But we tend to leave ministry to the so-called experts: the clergy. The New Testament, though, knows nothing of that division.

Neither does God. "And God said, 'I will be with you. And this will be the sign to you that it is I who have sent you: When you have brought the people out of Egypt, you will worship God on this mountain'" (3:12). God did not argue with Moses. He did not say, "There, there, Moses. You really are a special fellow, and much more talented than you give yourself credit for." He simply made two assertions: first, that Moses would not be facing down Pharaoh alone, for the Lord would be with him; and second, that Moses would see the fulfillment of this promise when all the Israelites gathered at Mount Sinai. When God calls us, he promises to go with us, however unqualified we may feel.

Moses' second objection had to do with *knowledge*. "Moses said to God, 'Suppose I go to the Israelites and say to them, "The God of your fathers has sent me to you," and they ask me, "What is his name?" Then what shall I tell them?'" (3:13). Moses was saying that he did not know enough to be an effective spokesman for the Lord. He was not theologically sophisticated or articulate. He did not even know God's proper name! If I'm going to stand before the Israelites, Moses might say, and claim that God appeared to me and commissioned me to confront Pharaoh, I had better be able to give the right answers when they ask some hard questions. I had better know more about God than the average guy in the pew. Otherwise, I'll come across as someone filled with a lot of hot air!

God was quite direct in his response. "God said to Moses, 'I AM WHO I AM. This is what you are to say to the Israelites: "I AM has sent me to you."' God also said to Moses, 'Say to the Israelites, "The LORD, the God of your fathers—the God of Abraham, the God of Isaac and the God of Jacob—has sent me to you"'" (3:14-15). The divine name "I AM" is connected with the verb "to be":

God *is* the source of all that exists. In our English Bibles, when we see "LORD" in capital letters, it translates "Yahweh," which "sounds like and may be derived from the Hebrew for *I AM*." (NIV footnote on 3:15).

God didn't want to be hidden. He didn't want his name to be a complicated or sophisticated thing. He said to Moses, in effect: You can know me and call me by name. He says the same to us as well. "I praise you, Father, Lord of heaven and earth," Jesus prayed, "because you have hidden these things from the wise and learned, and revealed them to little children. Yes, Father, for this was your good pleasure. All things have been committed to me by my Father. No one knows the Son except the Father, and no one knows the Father except the Son and those to whom the Son chooses to reveal him" (Matt 11:25-27). We do not need theological training to know God as one friend can know another. Indeed, God has come to us with a human face and name— Jesus. His call to us doesn't depend on our knowledge or our sophistication but on our love for him and our openness to his Spirit.

Third, Moses objected that he lacked *credibility*. "Moses answered, 'What if they do not believe me or listen to me and say, "The LORD did not appear to you"?'" (4:1). He was concerned— and rightly so—that the Israelites might consider him a religious maniac or a fraud. Remember that Moses was probably a well-known figure in the Hebrew community—he'd been raised "Egyptian" in Pharaoh's household; he ended up a killer after his feeble attempt to identify with the Hebrews; he fled into the desert to avoid arrest (see 2:11-15). So he wasn't a likely candidate for spiritual and political leader of the Israelites! Who would believe him? Knowing his background, his history, and his instability, who would take him seriously if he claimed to have had a vision of the Lord?

Often I wonder the same thing. Maybe you do too. Who will listen to me or take my profession of faith seriously? After all—I tell myself—my life is not always consistent with my faith. I can claim that I've surrendered my life to Jesus Christ, but my family and friends know better. They know the "real me": my temper, my laziness, my lack of concern when others are in pain, my—dare I say it?—hypocrisy. They might view my Christian claims suspiciously—and rightly so!

But God answered Moses' third objection dramatically: He performed two miracles. First, he transformed Moses' staff into a snake—and back again. Next, he made Moses' hand "leprous, like snow" (4:6), and then restored it again. God was sending a clear message to Moses: If anybody doubts the authenticity of your call, they'll be convinced when they see the Lord in action through your ministry.

The same process continues in our own lives. People often doubt a sinner's claims to conversion, but God deals with those doubts by working in and through the transformed person. At times, it's true, our Christian profession will lack credibility. The answer for us, as for Moses, is obedience—trusting that God will work through us.

Fourth, Moses objected that he lacked *competence* to serve the Lord. "Moses said to the LORD, 'O LORD, I have never been eloquent, neither in the past nor since you have spoken to your servant. I am slow of speech and tongue'" (4:10). He was probably right. We have to assume that Moses wasn't underestimating his abilities, that he knew himself well enough to affirm his weaknesses along with his strengths. His upbringing in the Egyptian court would have given him many opportunities to speak publicly, but he had discovered that he wasn't a "charismatic" personality or a spellbinding orator. The real Moses was probably nothing like Charlton Heston's towering— even overpowering—Moses in Cecil B. DeMille's *The Ten Commandments*. The reality seems to have been different. People would not have been drawn to him because of his persuasiveness. He didn't command attention. He wasn't what we would call a "gifted" individual.

Our own self-evaluations might be much like those of Moses. We're sure to know the gifts we *don't* possess. One person might say, "I'm not naturally gregarious." Another: "I'm not well-organized." Still another: "I get tongue tied when I try to speak in public," or "I fall apart whenever I go into a hospital to visit someone." We know, in other words, what we're *not* able to do.

But God doesn't really care about that. God accepts the reality of who we are but promises to overcome that reality through his power. "Then the LORD said to him, 'Who gives speech to mortals? Who makes them mute or deaf, seeing or blind? Is it not I, the LORD? Now go, and I will be with your mouth and teach you what you are to speak'" (4:11-12 NRSV). God claims the ability to override our disabilities; the ability to empower us for whatever task he calls us to. The New Testament is filled with this promise. "You will receive power when the Holy Spirit comes on you; and you will be my witnesses" (Acts 1:8). These were the words of Jesus just before he ascended to the Father. He spoke them to the same disciples (minus Judas) mentioned earlier: Peter, James and John, and the rest—people whose lack of competence and reliability had been proved in the events surrounding Jesus' arrest and death (Mark 14:50). Jesus promised them power and fulfilled the promise ten days later on Pentecost (Acts 2:1-11)—so awesomely that a huge crowd gathered and Peter preached. Peter, who just a few weeks before had denied knowing Jesus, now confronted thousands with the message: "This man [Jesus] was handed over to you by God's set purpose and foreknowledge; and *you,* with the help of wicked men, put him to death by nailing him to the cross" (Acts 2:23, italics mine). Three thousand people were baptized that day as a result of Peter's sermon. God empowered (and empowers) where natural abilities are lacking.

Moses' final objection is the one that really underlies them all: He didn't have the *will* to obey the Lord. "Moses said, 'O

LORD, please send someone else to do it'" (4:13). This is what he was getting at all along, isn't it? His true objection was unmasked. God had called him to a dangerous, all-consuming, thankless task, and he preferred not to be involved. He had no desire to return to Egypt and enter into battle with his foster family. Life in the desert may have been rigorous; but compared to the job to which he was called, it was relatively safe and secure.

In the end, the issue was not one of competence or credibility or anything of the sort. No, the issue had to do with Moses' willingness to obey. Will you, or won't you? This is our issue too. God is calling us into a relationship with Jesus Christ; calling us into the Christian community; calling us to serve Jesus concretely, daily, in every aspect of our life; calling us to listen for his voice and respond in obedience. And the question for us is the same as it was for Moses. Will you, or won't you? Only we can answer that question. No one can answer it for us.

God, understandably, had tired of Moses' objections. "Then the LORD's anger burned against Moses and he said, 'What about your brother, Aaron the Levite? I know he can speak well. He is already on his way to meet you, and his heart will be glad when he sees you. You shall speak to him and put words in his mouth; I will help both of you speak and will teach you what to do. . . . But take this staff in your hand so you can perform miraculous signs with it'" (4:14-15, 17). God made two promises: first, a helper, Moses' own brother, Aaron; and second, miraculous power, symbolized in the staff. Moses indeed obeyed—finally. But there's nothing in the text to tell us *why*. Ultimately, he just obeyed, period. This is what obedience is. We do what the Lord asks of us, even when we do not especially want to. "Come, follow me" (Mark 1:17), Jesus says, and then the choice is ours. Will you, Jesus asks, or won't you? Like Moses, like Andrea, our best response to God's call is to "Just do it."

Questions for Discussion

1. Moses struggled to justify himself for *not* obeying God's call. What objections do you raise when you sense that God may be calling you to service beyond your ability, your training, or your desire?

2. All of us have good reasons to believe that we're not "worthy" to serve the Lord. What are yours? How do you overcome them?

3. How has God strengthened you supernaturally when you thought you were "over your head" in responding to his call?

4. In the end, it came down to will: "O Lord, please send some-one else." Can you think of a time when you obeyed God even when you did not want to? What happened?

-4-

GOD'S CALL TO ORDINARY PEOPLE: BEZALEL AND OHOLIAB

Exodus 35:30-36:7

It was an age of superstars: God was calling leaders left and right. There was Moses, reluctant at first but in the end a powerful and dominant leader. Then there was Aaron the priest, Moses' brother, a gifted speaker and a dynamic if unreliable religious leader (Exod 32:1-6). And there was Miriam, sister of Moses and Aaron, a strong character and a singer and maker of songs (Exod 15:21). There was even an up-and-coming leader, young Joshua, Moses' attendant, a military commander destined forty years later to succeed his mentor.

Moses led well over a million Israelites out of Egypt, but only four superstars—Moses, Aaron, Miriam, and Joshua—were among them. What about the ordinary person? Where did he or she fit into God's plan? The Bible seems to present a few massive personalities and a massive number of "nonpersons." As we look at the call of a Moses or a Joshua, can we talk about God's call to unknown thousands listed in biblical genealogies? And what about God's call to us? I assume that most of us are ordinary, garden-variety people—not especially bad, not especially good, not especially anything. We try to be faithful to Jesus Christ, we try to reflect his love in our lives and his will in our obedience, but there is nothing spectacular about us. I am no Moses. You are probably no Miriam or Joshua.

Yet we too live in an age of superstars. The twentieth century has produced inspiring Christian heroes. Consider, for example, Dietrich Bonhoeffer, a Lutheran pastor and theologian hanged by the Nazis at the end of World War II. Before the war had even begun, he wrote, "When Christ calls a man, he bids him come and die."[1] Bonhoeffer lived—and died—his theology. Consider Terry Waite, envoy of the Archbishop of Canterbury, who spent five years as a hostage because he sought peace in Lebanon. Consider Martin Luther King Jr., a Christian whose courage deeply affected the conscience of a nation. Consider Billy Graham, the evangelist whose preaching has brought hundreds of thousands of people to Jesus Christ and who has carried on his ministry with integrity for almost six decades. Consider Anglican Archbishop Janani Luwum of Uganda, martyred for his opposition to Idi Amin's brutal regime. Consider Mother Theresa of Calcutta; her compassion touched the world, not only with the depth of her human love, but with the love of Jesus that infused it. Consider Archbishop Desmond Tutu, a powerful voice for reconciliation and hope in South Africa. Consider Christian authors C. S. Lewis and Dorothy Sayers, who have communicated the faith in a way that modern men and women can understand. Consider Pope John XXIII, elected as an old man to be a "caretaker pope," whose vision transformed not only the Roman Catholic Church but the entire Christian world. This is indeed an age of Christian giants; we live within living memory of men and women who will be honored centuries from now.

In light of these great men and women whom the Lord has raised up in our own day, what does God's call to *us* mean? Does God call ordinary, garden-variety people like us too? He surely did in the time of Moses. One of the tasks God gave to the Israelites encamped at the base of Mount Sinai was to build the tabernacle, a portable worship center that was to be the visible sign of the Lord's presence in the midst of his people. (The details are described in Exodus 25-31 and 35-40.) It was a grand project, but the men chosen to execute it were just ordinary guys. "Then Moses said to the Israelites: See, the LORD has called by name Bezalel son or Uri son of Hur, of the tribe of Judah . . . and Oholiab son of Ahisamach, of the tribe of Dan" (35:30, 34 NRSV). These two men didn't volunteer for the work. They were chosen—called by God. What kind of people were they? Today we'd call them skilled craftsmen—blue-collar workers. They weren't leaders, religious or political. They had no public role in the Israelite community—they were ordinary people who did ordinary jobs. In fact, the particular ministry they were commissioned to do flowed directly from the skills and talents they employed in their work. Their job in "real life" was to construct things; when God called them, it was construction he had in mind. But their task was a *calling* from the Lord. It may have been "ordinary," but it was divinely ordered.

Most of us are like Bezalel and Oholiab: neither leaders nor superstars in the Christian community, ordinary people with ordinary jobs, equipped with ordinary gifts and talents. *Yet we also are called!* The Letter to the Hebrews says that all of us who belong to Jesus Christ "share in the heavenly calling" (3:1). Consider the apostolic band, the twelve whom Jesus specially chose to accompany and learn from him. They were mostly "Bezalel and Oholiab" type of people; there were no rabbis among them, no scholars, no members of the hereditary Jewish priesthood. Consider too how many of the New Testament letters end with personal greetings to ordinary Christians. "Greet Rufus, chosen in the Lord; and greet his mother—a mother to me also. Greet Asyncritus, Phlegon, Hermes, Patrobas, Hermas, and the brothers and sisters who are with them" (Rom 16:13-14 NRSV). Paul had a high regard for the ordinary, "standard brand" Christian. Indeed, the word "saints" (see 1 Cor 1:2; 2 Cor 1:1; Eph 1:1; et al.) simply means "holy ones." We are all holy because we have been called by Jesus, set apart for his service.

The Christian Church has been recovering the notion of "every-member ministry." This has been a great blessing to the Christian community, because it has released the gifts and talents of ordinary Christians and put them to use for the Lord. Unfortunately, the concept of every-member ministry is sometimes misunderstood. Two misconceptions stand out. First, some think of every-member ministry as laypeople doing part of the clergy's job. The clergy, of course, have a highly public ministry—they preach and teach, they lead a congregation, they shepherd the hurt and the broken, they preside at the celebration of the sacraments. There is nothing in these tasks—beyond the sacramental—that requires an ordained person, so sharing with the laity the ministries of teaching or pastoral care, for example, is often an excellent idea. But if every-member ministry simply means doing "preacher-esque" jobs, then only a small number of laypersons—those with a more public set of gifts and talents—will offer themselves. Every-member ministry must mean more than doing what the ordained minister does.

Second, some think of every-member ministry exclusively in terms of the institutional church. They may look for a job within the church—working on a committee, caring for buildings and grounds, directing finances, or singing in the choir—and label it "my ministry." They confine their search for ministry to a job within the congregation. By definition, though, there will always be more members than there are jobs to go around. If we limit every-member ministry to jobs within the church, it becomes a narrow concept indeed. It must mean more than that.

Think of it this way instead: Every-member ministry is living out whatever you are doing for the sake of Jesus Christ, whether the task is within the church or well beyond it. When Christians carry on their ordinary occupations for Jesus' sake, doing their best to show the love of Jesus to their customers or supervisors or coworkers, that occupation becomes part of their ministry. When Christians raise their children to know and love Jesus, seeking to impart to them the values of the kingdom of God, parenting becomes part of their ministry. Our daily calling becomes a divine calling when it's offered to Jesus. Every-member ministry involves the conscious decision to make an impact on our world for Jesus Christ, and "our world" includes our home, neighborhood, workplace, school—and church.

Every Christian has a ministry. For some, that ministry is exclusively within the context of the church. For others, it is exclusively beyond it. For still others, it may include both the institutional church and the world outside. Bezalel and Oholiab made their occupation as craftsmen available to the Lord. In so doing, the "ordinary" became a vehicle for God's extraordinary purpose. This principle is true for us as well.

I find myself thinking about "ordinary" Christians who have touched my life. The list is as awe-inspiring to me as my list of twentieth-century Christian heroes. Here's one example: Consider Jerry, a retired pharmacist. He's a small man, hardly more than five feet tall, with a giant heart for Jesus. Thirty years ago he helped to organize a prayer group at All Saints, Bakersfield, California, a prayer group that still meets every Tuesday night. Thousands of lives have been enriched by their prayers. Consider Martha, a registered nurse who works such long hours that her only real contact with the church is Sunday morning worship. "I can't do much for the parish," she once told me. "I don't have time. But whenever I go into a patient's room I pray for him or her—usually silently, under my breath, and they don't even know that I'm doing it. The funny thing is, time after time I've seen patients I've prayed for being discharged early— they get well so fast!" Consider Walt, a carpenter and a handy- man by trade, whose truck is a wonder to behold. The back of his pickup is a horrendous jumble of tools, parts, wires, odd-sized pieces of wood, screws, nails, all piled together in no discernable order. I became something of a project of his. Some people are all thumbs. I am worse: I am all elbows. When something went wrong in my house, I always called Walt. He would pull up in his truck, survey the problem, reach down into the jumble for exact- ly the right part or tool—and the problem would be fixed in a moment. Why did he do that? Because he loves Jesus, loves his priest, and wants to offer the best that he has to God. God has called each of these three friends of mine to a unique ministry, just as he called Bezalel and Oholiab. And after a call, God never leaves anyone stranded. When God singled out Bezalel and Oholiab to build the tabernacle, he equipped them in three ways for the task.

First, God gave them the spiritual power and the gifts and talents they would need. The Lord filled Bezalel "with the Spirit of God, with skill, ability and knowledge in all kinds of crafts. . . . And he has given both him and Oholiab son of Ahisamach, of the tribe of Dan, the ability to teach others. He has filled them with skill to do all kinds of work as craftsmen, designers, embroiderers in blue, purple and scarlet yarn and fine linen, and weavers" (Exod 35:31, 34-35). God did not leave Bezalel and Oholiab to their own devices. He gave them, above all, the Holy Spirit, God's indwelling power. He gave them the particular set of skills they would require for the job. He does the same for us. All our skills—"the natural" talents we were born with or the abilities that seem to come almost supernaturally later in life — come from God. Each of us has a unique combination of abilities that enables us to do the very things the Lord calls us to do.

Second, God gave Bezalel and Oholiab companions in ministry. "So Bezalel, Oholiab and every skilled person to whom the LORD has given skill and ability to know how to carry out all the work of constructing the sanctuary are to do the work just as the LORD commanded" (Exod 36:1). They weren't to carry out their task alone. God provided coworkers—a gaggle of craftsmen! This is an important principle. Christians often conceive of ministry as a solitary activity, but the Scriptures paint a different picture. "Calling the Twelve to him, [Jesus] sent them out two by two and gave them authority over evil spirits" (Mark 6:7). Later, Jesus dispatched a larger group of followers. "The Lord appointed seventy-two others and sent them two by two ahead of him to

every town and place where he was about to go" (Luke 10:1).
Jesus spent much of his time preparing his immediate followers
for ministry. He used a variety of methods: demonstration (they
watched him at work), teaching (Matthew 10 provides a good
example of how Jesus taught his disciples to do what he did),
practical experience (the ministry excursions already mentioned), and reflection (in Luke 10:17-20, Jesus and the seventy-
two discuss what had happened on their mission). The whole
process was suffused with community. Neither Jesus nor his
disciples ministered alone.

Nor should we. Even ministry that appears to be solitary
should flow out of our life in the Christian community. For
example, as I sit writing this chapter, I am alone. There is no one
in the room with me; I am staring into the inhuman face of a
computer screen. And yet this book is the product of community life. Each chapter has its origin in a sermon: My brothers and
sisters and I together wrestled with some aspect of God's call.
Then the congregation provided me with the time (a sabbatical)
and the equipment (the computer) to turn sparse sermon notes
into prose. So an activity that seems highly individual on the
surface has really been made possible by the community.
Without their attention, comments, prayers, and gifts of time
and technology, I would not be here writing. In fact, without
them I would have nothing helpful to say, because I would not
have acquired the ministry experience that has made the biblical
principles come alive for me.

*Third, God provided the resources they needed for their
task.* Even before God called Bezalel and Oholiab to build the
tabernacle, Moses had asked the Israelites for contributions of
gold, silver, and bronze, yarn and linen, skins, wood, and other
materials. "And they came, everyone whose heart was stirred, and
everyone whose spirit was willing, and brought the LORD's
offering to be used for the tent of meeting, and for all its service,
and for the sacred vestments" (Exod 35:21 NRSV). After Bezalel

and Oholiab were appointed, the people "continued to bring freewill offerings morning after morning. So all the skilled craftsmen who were doing all the work on the sanctuary left their work and said to Moses, 'The people are bringing more than enough for doing the work the LORD commanded to be done'" (36:3-5). Bezalel and Oholiab discovered that when God commissions a task, he always provides the resources, material and spiritual, to accomplish it. He had provided personnel and skills; now he supplied the material requirements as well.

God is gracious, not only in calling us to Christ and his service, but also in enabling us to obey. He graciously gives us gifts and talents and abilities, companions for the task, and resources beyond our imagining or deserving. Paul saw this principle in action when he asked the Christians in Corinth to take up a collection to benefit poorer brothers and sisters in Judea. God, he says, even supplies resources so that we can have a ministry of giving resources away. "You will be made rich in every way so that you can be generous on every occasion, and through us your generosity will result in thanksgiving to God" (2 Cor 9:11). And then a note of gratitude to the one who made this possible: "Thanks be to God for his indescribable gift!" (9:15).

---

[1] Dietrich Bonhoeffer, *The Cost of Discipleship* (New York: Macmillan, 1959).

Questions for Discussion

1.   Christians today suffer from a "superstar" mentality, a tendency made more pronounced by the growth of Christian radio and television. How has this tendency affected your view of yourself and your own ministry?

2.   Bezalel and Oholiab remind us of ordinary Christians everywhere, people unpretentious yet gifted. Can you think of people like this in your own experience? How has God used them to touch your life?

3.   What are the talents—perhaps the less spectacular talents—that the Lord has given you? In what ways have you used them for ministry?

4.   Who are your companions in ministry? Who are the people whose advice, assistance, and presence are essential as you serve the Lord?

-5-

THE FEAR OF GOD'S CALL: JOSHUA

Joshua 1:1-9

The first time I walked down a jetway after the September 11 attacks—eight days later, to be exact—I kept replaying in my mind an "endless loop" video of the horror: planes slamming into the World Trade Center, collapsing buildings, a charred gash in the side of the Pentagon, people fleeing lower Manhattan as debris showered down on them, a crater in the Pennsylvania countryside. Try as I might, I couldn't erase those scenes from my mind. I imagined myself in one of those planes, screaming earthward. I imagined the sights, the sounds, the emotions of immanent destruction. My heart rate and my sweating palms gave physical expression to fear.

We can't talk ourselves out of fear, I discovered that day. We can't dismiss it with a smile, a joke, or a song. Fear seems to have a power of its own. It can take over our thought life, dominate our decisions, and even immobilize our faith. Fear can also affect our ability to hear and obey God's call. "Do not be afraid, Mary" (Luke 1:30), the angel Gabriel said at the Annunciation, knowing that fear could prevent Mary from saying the yes that would change the course of history. "Do not be afraid" (Matt 28:10), Jesus said at the tomb on the first Easter morning, freeing the women to tell the good news that the Lord was risen. "Do not be afraid." But how can we be released from our fears so that we can answer the Lord's call?

Take a look at Joshua—he was a man who had every reason to be afraid. With his fellow Israelites, he was camped on the east bank of the Jordan River. For forty years, under Moses' leadership, they'd wandered through the Sinai desert, capturing the territory that would later be known as the Trans-Jordan (Num 21:21-35). But the main goal of their march—the heart of the promised land, west of the Jordan—was still in the hands of Canaanite tribes. From this camp east of the Jordan, "Moses climbed Mount Nebo. . . . There the LORD showed him the whole land" (Deut 34:1), from Galilee in the north to the Negev in the south, from the Jordan in the east to the Mediterranean Sea in the west. "Then the LORD said to him, 'This is the land I promised on oath to Abraham, Isaac and Jacob when I said, "I will give it to your descendants." I have let you see it with your eyes, but you will not cross over into it.' And Moses the servant of the LORD died there in Moab" (34:4-5). Someone else would lead the Israelites into the promised land: Joshua son of Nun.

The Book of Joshua begins as God restates Joshua's call. In many ways, the call says as much about Joshua as it does about the Lord. Over and over the Lord told Joshua to be brave. "Be strong and courageous. . . . Be strong and very courageous. . . . Be strong and courageous. Do not be terrified; do not be discouraged, for the LORD your God will be with you wherever you go" (Josh 1:6, 7, 9). I am working from a basic assumption: When the Lord repeats something that often, he is underlining a point, putting it in bold print. Why would God have to tell Joshua over and over not to be afraid? Because Joshua was frightened—and for good reason.

First, Joshua now carried the burden of leadership for the entire Israelite nation. For forty years he had been able to refer problems up the administrative ladder. "I'm sorry," he might say, "you'll have to talk to Moses about that." Even the most influential assistant can't fully comprehend the stress that comes with being in charge. But now the shekel stopped with Joshua. He was responsible—solely responsible—for a community that had consistently grumbled, sinned, rebelled.

Second, the task Joshua faced—leading the Israelites in driving out the indigenous peoples of Canaan—was both dangerous and impossibly difficult. These peoples were numerous and technologically advanced; they lived in fortified cities. We have the benefit of hindsight—we know what God did to a city like Jericho (Josh 6:20-21). Joshua, however, did not know this as he listened to God restate his call. All he knew was that he faced potentially huge battle losses and, if his generalship failed, humiliating defeat. Dag Hammarskjold, Secretary General of the United Nations until his death in a plane crash in 1960, expressed the burden of his office: "Your responsibility is indeed terrifying. If you fail, it is God, thanks to your having betrayed Him, who will fail mankind. You fancy you can be responsible *to* God; can you carry the responsibility *for* God?"[1] Perhaps Joshua felt that kind of burden, and the fear that goes with it, as he gazed across the Jordan at the promised land.

Fear is a specifically human problem, the inevitable result of one of God's most gracious gifts—the gift of time. We experience time in three modes: We can look back at the past, we can speculate about the future (often on the basis of what we remember from the past), and we can live in the present—all at once. This is a gift. It gives us perspective, a sense of history, and the ability to plan and dream. Unfortunately, it also enables us to experience fear. As we look into the future, we can imagine not only the good things but also the terrifying things that might happen. Time allows us both to fantasize and to visualize catastrophe. And when we face danger, memory kicks in. We think about a similar situation in the past and imagine what that might portend for the future.

Marlowe, the narrator of Joseph Conrad's novel *Lord Jim*, describes the state of mind of a young mariner who believes that his ship is about to sink. "He was not afraid of death perhaps, but I'll tell you what, he was afraid of the emergency. His confounded imagination had evoked for him all the horrors of panic, the trampling rush, the pitiful screams, boats swamped—all the appalling incidents of a disaster at sea he had ever heard of. He might have been resigned to die, but I suspect he wanted to die without added terrors, quietly, in a sort of peaceful trance."[2] Our own fears are like that. Whatever we're afraid of—flying, dentists, spiders, speaking in public, sharing our faith—the fear is more acute because in our mind's eye we can already "see" the disaster to come.

Joshua, looking across the Jordan toward that dangerous promised land, could imagine the terrors of battle, the dreadful stillness of death and defeat. "Be strong and courageous, Joshua," the Lord said, and Joshua needed to hear it. As he restated Joshua's call, God said three things that spoke directly to Joshua's fear.

First, act on God's promises. God said, "Moses my servant is dead. Now then, you and all these people, get ready to cross the Jordan River into the land I am about to give to them—to the Israelites. I will give you every place where you set your foot, as I promised Moses. . . . No one will be able to stand up against you all the days of your life. As I was with Moses, so I will be with you; I will never leave you nor forsake you" (Josh 1:2-3, 5). God makes two promises here: the promise of conquest and the promise of his sustaining presence. There was, in the end, only one way for Joshua to discover if it was truly in God's plan for the Israelites to occupy Canaan. He had to step out on the basis of what God had promised him. There was no shortcut, no "trial balloon." Only one option was available: Gather the people together and cross the Jordan. See what God would do.

God's promises are like that. They are tested in the doing. What God requires is our yes to Jesus, and that yes is part of God's answer to our fears.

Second, obey God's law. "Be careful to obey all the law my servant Moses gave you; do not turn from it to the right or to the left, that you may be successful wherever you go" (Josh 1:7). God had revealed his law to Moses on Mount Sinai. The law included both ceremonial regulations that ordered Israel's worship and moral commandments that dealt with Israel's relationship with God and with one another. The Ten Commandments (Exod 20:1-17; Deut 5:6-21) are in the latter category. Obedience to God involved submission to his law, and God reminded Joshua that obedience was a precondition to blessing.

Christians are not exempt from this command to obey. Sometimes we mistakenly contrast law and grace and classify obedience as a subcategory of law. We call it legalism—an attempt to win God's favor by doing religious acts. But obedience isn't keeping God's rules and regulations. It's our response to what God has already done for us in Jesus Christ. Jesus said, "If you love me, you will obey what I command" (John 14:15). Obedience is the natural working out of Jesus' love for us and our love for him. Nor do we obey simply out of our own strength. Six hundred years before Jesus' birth, the prophet Jeremiah heard God saying, "I will put my law within them, and I will write it on their hearts; and I will be their God, and they shall be my people. No longer shall they teach one another, or say to each other, 'Know the LORD,' for they shall all know me, from the least of them to the greatest" (Jer 31:33-34 NRSV). In this passage, God promises a new basis for conduct. The law will no longer be simply an external set of demands. God will carve his will deep within us; through his indwelling Spirit we will *want* to obey what Jesus commands.

The conversion of St. Augustine of Hippo (354-430 C.E.) came down to a struggle between obedience and rebellion, which he describes in his autobiography, *The Confessions*.

> I kept saying to myself, 'Now! Now!' and had myself just about talked into it; but not quite. I took a deep breath and tried again, and each time came a little closer, and a little closer, so I could almost reach out and take hold of it. But I couldn't hold it or even touch it, because I hesitated to take the step that

would make me die to death and live to life." In the
garden of a friend's home, "I heard a voice coming
from the house next door. Whether it was a boy's or a
girl's I don't know, but it was singing over and over in
a kind of chant, 'Take up and read, take up and read!'
. . . I could only interpret the words as a kind of divine
command to open the Scripture and read the first
passage I came across. . . . Now I grabbed the book
[a volume of Paul's letters], opened it, and read silently the first portion of Scripture on which my eyes
lighted: 'Not in reveling and drunkenness, not in
debauchery and licentiousness, not in quarreling and
jealousy. But put on the Lord Jesus Christ, and make
no provision for the flesh, to gratify its desires' [Rom
13:13-14]. I had no need or wish to read further, for
when I came to the end of the sentence, instantly, it
seemed, a light of certainty turned on in my heart and
all the fog of doubt disappeared."[3]

God's call to Augustine, transforming his doubt, hinged on
obedience—his willingness to let the Spirit change him from
within. God's call to us hinges on that same obedience. As we
obey, we see our fears are transformed too, and we see them in a
new light.

Third, remember God's deeds. "Do not let this Book of the
Law depart from your mouth; meditate on it day and night"
(Josh 1:8). The phrase "Book of the Law" means more than
simply the law codes found in Exodus, Leviticus, Numbers, and
Deuteronomy. The codes are set in a larger framework: the story
of God's dealings with his people, from the creation of the world
and humankind's rebellion, to the call of Abraham and the
patriarchs, to the sojourn in Egypt, the exodus, and the wander-
ings in the desert. As God's people remembered how the Lord
had lovingly cared for them in the past, they would be given

strength to face their fears about the future. Their "meditation" would remind them of God's love and faithfulness, of the basic trustworthiness of the God who commanded them to cross the Jordan and take the promised land.

In the New Testament too, as God's people take that same look backward at the Lord's faithfulness, they gather strength to walk forward with him into the unknown future. "Everything that was written in the past," St. Paul tells us, "was written to teach us, so that through endurance and the encouragement of the Scriptures we might have hope" (Rom 15:4).

Thirty years ago, when I was a very young and very inexperienced assistant in a parish, a little boy named Jesse was rushed to the hospital and diagnosed with meningitis encephalitis—meningitis not in the spine but, even worse, within the head. Jesse's brain was swollen, and he lay in a deep coma. Day after day I joined the parishioners who visited Jesse's parents, Jeff and Nancy, as they kept vigil in the hospital. We sat with them, said words of comfort, prayed, sometimes just remained silent. Two days, five days, eight days, ten days—time passed, and Jesse didn't wake up. The doctors seemed to be avoiding Jesse's parents; there was nothing useful or hopeful for them to say. One afternoon as my visit with Jeff and Nancy ended, we were standing around the hospital crib. We held hands and prayed. Then, almost instinctively—we had not done so until this point—we laid our hands together on Jesse's head. Someone prayed aloud; I do not remember who spoke, whether it was one of the parents or myself. But the prayer was basic and desperate. "God, please make Jesse well. In Jesus' name. Amen." That, and nothing more. I put on my coat and left. When I walked in the door at home, the phone was ringing. It was Jeff, calling to tell me that as soon as I had left the room, Jesse had awakened, with no warning or fanfare. Over the following days, the doctors announced to their amazement that there was no apparent brain damage, none of the after-effects they expected to find if the child woke up at all.

This story isn't especially unusual. In the years since, I've seen God heal many times. But after Jesse's healing, I went through a long and horrendous "dry" time, lasting nearly five years. Nothing seemed to be happening in my life and ministry. I was afraid that it was all for naught, that I was wasting my time. I preached and counseled and celebrated the sacraments and taught—to what purpose? I didn't know. Eventually the Lord brought me through this darkness and beyond, into refreshment and renewal. But during those five years, when the fear and the doubt were at their worse, I would look back at Jesse's healing and remember God's deeds. Time after time, it was this memory that enabled me to trust that Jesus really *is* Lord, that he does indeed reign not only over heaven and earth in general but also over my life in particular. Part of God's antidote for Joshua's fear was the command to look backward at the ways that the Lord had dealt with his people. I've discovered that this look backward—not in mere nostalgia but in faith—is an antidote for my fear as well. "I will never leave you or forsake you" (Josh 1:5).

---

[1] Dag Hammarskjold, *Markings* (New York: Knopf, 1968), 155.

[2] Joseph Conrad, *Lord Jim* (Boston: Houghton Mifflin, 1958), 65.

[3] Quoted in Sherwood Elliot Wirt, *Love Story: Augustine's Confessions for Modern Man* (New York: Harper and Row, 1971), 116–18.

Questions for Discussion

1.   What triggers a response of fear in you? Does the gift of time—and our ability to gaze into an unknown future and speculate it—help or hinder you as you deal with fear?

2.   Joshua's fears (the burden of leadership, the dangers and difficulties of his task) threatened to overwhelm his ministry. How have you experienced these fears in your life?

3.   How have you lived out the challenge of obedience in the face of fear, even legitimate fear? Augustine's life was transformed, finally, when he read Romans 13:13-14. Is there a biblical commandment that has similarly transformed you?

4.   Think of ways in which God has acted powerfully in your life—a moment of spiritual insight, a time of healing, an encounter with the Lord's saving grace. How can these memories assist you in the midst of fear?

-6-

CALLED BY A COMMUNITY: DEBORAH

Judges 4:1-5:31

When God calls my name, will I recognize his voice? Even though I come closer to Christ, eager to do his will, how can I know for sure what that is? How can I know that he's talking to *me?* All of us yearn for something—perhaps an audible voice, perhaps a sign in the sky. We listen oh so carefully, and nothing happens.

Years ago, for example, a congregation invited me to become its rector. I debated the merits of the call, lined up the pros and cons, looked at the opportunities for developing my ministry in a new direction, and considered the drawbacks of moving my family and starting over someplace else. I pondered the Bible, read passages like Isaiah 43:1 ("Fear not, for I have redeemed you; I have summoned you by name; you are mine"), prayed, and listened. Silence. No hint of God's voice. One day, in desperation, I paced around a local park, determined to encounter some sign of the divine summons. Maybe out here in nature, amid trees and grass and birds and pond and clear blue sky, God would speak. He didn't—or if he did, I failed to hear him. "Truly you are a God who hides himself," Isaiah said (45:15), half in awe and half in frustration. That day, I could readily agree!

Sometimes, though, God's voice comes to us through the words and actions of others. Often we discern his call not through the "gentle whisper" in our hearts (1 Kgs 19:12) but through the invitation of a community. Such was the case with Deborah, prophet and judge.

In the centuries following the death of Joshua, the Israelites

had no central government. They were at best a loose confederacy of tribes dealing with the threat of peoples both within
Canaan and just outside its borders. There were Moabites,
Canaanites, Midianites, Amalekites, Ammonites, Philistines, and
"other eastern peoples" (Judg 6:3) who would periodically
attack. With no central authority to appeal to for help, the
Israelites found another solution. Temporary military-political
leaders called judges arose and rallied the Israelites to repel their
enemies. These judges, though, were only a short-term response
to the problem. When the enemy had been defeated and the
crisis passed, the judges went back to their ordinary lives.

Israel's crises weren't just military. They were spiritual as
well. Before they arrived in Canaan, the Israelites had been
commanded sternly and repeatedly not to worship the gods of
the peoples whose territory they were about to invade. But the
temptation was nearly impossible for them to resist.

As you read the Book of Judges, you'll see a pattern appear.
First, the Israelites would do "evil in the eyes of the LORD" (Judg
3:12 et al.) by worshiping other gods. Then God, in anger, would
send a hostile neighbor to attack and oppress the Israelites as
punishment for their apostasy. And when the Israelites "cried out
to the LORD" (3:15 et al.), God would raise up a judge who led the
Israelite tribes, drove out the enemy, and restored peace. The
cycle would repeat: apostasy, oppression, repentance and a cry
for help, and another gracious act of deliverance. This is the
pattern into which the ministry of Deborah fits.

For Deborah, hearing God's voice was a three-stage
process. *It began with a crisis.* "The LORD sold [the Israelites] into
the hands of Jabin, a king of Canaan, who reigned in Hazor. The
commander of his army was Sisera. . . . Because he had nine
hundred iron chariots and had cruelly oppressed the Israelites
for twenty years, they cried to the LORD for help" (4:2-3). The
Israelites faced a disaster both military and spiritual. Their
enemies the Canaanites, technologically advanced with superior

weapons and a renowned commander, out-manned and out-gunned them. No wonder Canaanite oppression lasted twenty years!

But lurking below the surface of military catastrophe was an even grimmer reality. God had abandoned the Israelites again—and deservedly so, for they seemed incapable of maintaining single-minded devotion to the Lord. The lure of a foreign and exotic religion, complete with a fertility cult and ritual prostitution, tempted them away from the austere and demanding God of the desert. Finally, the crisis of Canaanite military action triggered a plea for help. Their sincerity may have been questionable, but the Israelites knew their only hope was in the living God. Military and spiritual disaster thrust them into the arms of the Lord.

Crises in our lives often impel profound questions too. What is God doing? What does he want with me? What is he trying to say to me through these agonizing events? How can I hear his voice? The crisis may be personal, vocational, familial; as varied as a runaway child, a failed business, or a loss of confidence that I am living my life the way God intends.

Stan, for example, spent much of his professional career designing "smart bombs" for a huge aerospace firm. Throughout the 1980s and into the 90s, Stan devoted himself to producing accurate and effective weaponry—until, that is, his company lost the contract. Suddenly, at age 58, Stan found himself unemployed. He had spent his whole life as an aerospace engineer, and the past fifteen years on a specific project. Could he start over now? More painfully, should he even try? He found himself asking difficult questions. Did God intend something different for the rest of his life? What was the Lord's call? How could Stan hear God? It was crisis that drove Stan to cry out for help.

A crisis isn't necessarily a bad thing. On the contrary, it may force us into a listening mode, making us more receptive to hearing God's voice. The Lord doesn't send misery into our lives simply to drive us into his arms—the reality is more complicated in our fallen, broken world, where crises just happen. Sometimes crises may be self-induced, as they were with the Israelites and their dabbling in alternative religions, but more often they simply occur, and their origin is wrapped in mystery. Whatever their root, crises can present an opportunity. James can tell us, "My brothers and sisters, whenever you face trials of any kind, consider it nothing but joy, because you know that the testing of your faith produces endurance; and let endurance have its full effect, so that you may be mature and complete, lacking in nothing" (Jas 1:2-4 NRSV).

The second stage for Deborah in hearing God's voice involved the community. We know virtually nothing about Deborah's background. By the time we meet her, she is already a judge. "Deborah, a prophetess, the wife of Lappidoth, was leading Israel at that time. She held court under the Palm of Deborah between Ramah and Bethel in the hill country of Ephraim, and the Israelites came to her to have their disputes decided" (4:4-5). The story of Deborah is told twice: in Judges 4, in prose; and in Judges 5, repeated (with minor variations) in poetry, often called the Song of Deborah. Thus the poem adds: "Then the people of the LORD went down to the city gates. 'Wake up, wake up, Deborah! Wake up, wake up, break out in song!'" (5:11-12). People instinctively trusted Deborah. Today we would say that she had "leadership quality," that combination of charisma, vision, graciousness, and personal strength that causes someone to rise to the top of an organization. When crisis erupted on the Canaanite front, people simply knew that Deborah was the one to lead them. Deborah heard no audible voice, saw no dramatic sign. God called to her through the voices of her neighbors.

That's how it was for Margaret. She believed deeply that she had discovered God's will for her life. As a college student she had pursued a lifelong dream to be a high school physical education teacher. By the time I met her, she'd been teaching in a local high school for a decade. She had coached the girls' basketball team to several regional championships and had married and become a mother. She had no plans to change the direction of her life—until she began to notice an unexpected phenomenon. Over several years, she realized, her students would linger after school to talk, to unload their problems, to seek advice. Young women intuitively knew that Margaret was someone they could trust. She never thought of herself as a counselor—indeed, the school had staff officially designated for that role. But over time Margaret came to sense that God had a new call for her. The fact that students sought her out for wisdom and guidance preyed more and more on her heart and mind, and finally, even painfully, she recognized God's voice. She left her teaching position, earned a master's degree in counseling, and now works full-time as a Christian psychotherapist—all because a community of young women came to her and asked for advice.

It is often a community that articulates the heart of God, gives it decibels, makes it explicit. This was certainly the case when the Israelites turned to Deborah as she sat under a palm tree (4:5). It was the case for Margaret. And it's often the case with us as well.

Finally, Deborah recognized God's call and immediately moved into action. "She sent for Barak son of Abinoam from Kedesh in Naphtali and said to him, 'The LORD, the God of Israel, commands you: "Go, take with you ten thousand men of Naphtali and Zebulon and lead the way to Mount Tabor. I will lure Sisera, the commander of Jabin's army, with his chariots and his troops to the Kishon River and give him into your hands"'" (4:6-7). Some people, including some Israelite tribes, were reluctant to follow Deborah and join the fight (5:16-18). Barak, apparently frightened by the prospect of facing nine hundred chariots, insisted that Deborah accompany him into battle. Deborah agreed but warned, "Because of the way you are going about this, the honor will not be yours, for the LORD will hand

Sisera over to a woman" (4:9).

In the end, however, Israel defeated Sisera, thanks to a combination of military strategy (4:14-16) and cooperative weather (5:20-21). Sisera fled, taking refuge in the tent of a woman named Jael, who fulfilled Deborah's prophecy by driving a tent peg through the head of the sleeping Canaanite general (5:26-27). The poet adds, "So may all your enemies perish, O LORD!" (5:31). A grim business, admittedly; but once more, God's people have been rescued because someone answered the Lord's call.

The community articulates God's call in two directions. *First, we hear God's call through others.* This is not, of course, an infallible process. Even people with the best of intentions can give us bad advice. We must exercise discernment, search the Scriptures, "test the spirits to see whether they are from God" (1 John 4:1). If a committee of Christians informed me that it's God's will that rob a bank, I wouldn't need to pray about the issue to discern its wrongheadedness. There is a relevant commandment (Exod 20:15) that tells me the advice is contrary to the revealed will of God. On the other hand, the areas of our lives for which we seek God's will are often those in which there is no specific scriptural guidance: whether to marry and whom to marry; which vocation to choose; how to share our faith in the workplace; where to live; which ministry invitations to accept (and which to decline!). Fellow Christians often help us to clarify issues, ask relevant questions, and look at alternative courses of action. The community provides an "atmosphere of discernment" that helps us to hear God's voice.

Christians can create that kind of atmosphere quite unconsciously. My friend and former parishioner Joy, for example, writes letters almost constantly. She writes everyone—on their birthdays, on their anniversaries, when there is no particular occasion at all—letters of encouragement, with some variation of "Jesus loves you and I love you." Over and over people have told me that a letter from Joy has come just when they needed to be reminded that God holds them in his heart. Over and over Joy's letters remind me that I am called, chosen, beloved by the Lord. Joy is for me a sign of what the Christian community should be doing day by day: encouraging, challenging, "spur[ring] one another on toward love and good deeds" (Heb 10:24).

Second, we articulate God's call to others. Sometimes, without even being aware of the fact, we can say the word or ask the question that has the potential of transforming another person's life. A few years ago, for example, my wife and I were on vacation in San Diego. On Sunday we worshiped at a nearby Episcopal church, I in "civvies" and enjoying the anonymity. When the service was over and Sylvia and I headed for the door, I heard a voice from the other side of the church. "Father Ed . . . Father Ed!" My heart sank. *There is no escape,* I thought. A woman rushed up to us, a stranger, or so it seemed. "Don't you remember me?" she asked. I searched my memory banks and came up empty. "No," I confessed, "I'm afraid I don't." "I visited your former parish a couple of times ten or twelve years ago," she reminded me. "Those visits changed my life." She had my attention! "Up until that time, I was a nominal Christian—I went to church on Christmas and Easter, but I never took Jesus seriously. Then on a business trip I spent a couple of weeks in Buena Park"—the location of my former parish—"and I had nothing to do on Sunday morning, so I came to St. Joseph's. You said something in your sermon that has affected me from that day to this." She went on to detail what I had said that morning, illustrations and all. In honesty, I must admit that I don't remember the sermon or anything specific about her visit. But something I had said triggered something in her, and Jesus touched her heart.

The community speaks God's word to us, yes; but we in turn can speak it to others. Chance conversations can change people's lives. We are always "on call," and our words have power beyond our imagining. The people who streamed to the Palm of Deborah couldn't have dreamed that they were the very mouth-piece of the living God, yet their cry for help mobilized Deborah, who mobilized God's people, once more defeating the enemy. We can recognize in others truths they cannot see for themselves— hidden strengths, gifts, talents, a spiritual reservoir of enormous promise. The key is our willingness to speak that word of encouragement and challenge that, even unknown to us, can unveil the heart of God.

Questions for Discussion

1.   What crises in your life have set you on a quest for God's will? What was the result? What did you discover about God's call?

2.   The community of Israel came to Deborah and summoned her to leadership. How have others articulated God's call to you? How did you recognize God's voice through their very human voices?

3.   When Deborah heard God's call, she immediately moved into action. Are there any actions that the Lord may be impelling you to embark on today?

4.   As you think about your own Christian community, whom may the Lord be calling you to encourage? How can you be God's spokesperson for that friend?

-7-

GOD'S CALL AND OUR SELF-IMAGE: GIDEON

Judges 6:1-40

When you look at yourself, what do you see? If you see someone who's useful, competent, strong—someone who can spring to action in a crisis—then you'll probably respond with a yes when God calls you to a challenge. On the other hand, if you look in the mirror and see somebody who's useless, incompetent, weak—a basket case in times of crisis —then you just might say no when God's call stretches you to try something new or difficult. Self-image is a big part of the Christian life.

Self-image is the result of many factors: what your parents and friends told you when you were a child, your performance in school and your teachers' and parents' response, and even the general "climate" of your childhood—was it affirming or condemning, warm or emotionally chilly? Your self-image continues to be formed as an adult by your successes and failures in work, love, sports, and even the church. It's formed by the kind of people you surround yourself with and what they say about you.

The question you face as a Christian is this: How do you view yourself, and what impact does that view have on your response to the call of God? Let's consider that question by looking at Gideon, one of the Bible's most complex characters.

When we first meet Gideon, the Israelites are once again in a sorry state. "Again the Israelites did evil in the eyes of the LORD, and for seven years he gave them into the hands of the Midianites" (Judg 6:1), who invaded Israelite country, ruined their crops, stole their livestock, and forced the Israelites to hide in caves. We're back to the familiar pattern of the previous chapter. "Midian so impoverished the Israelites that they cried out to the LORD for help" (6:6). God first sent a prophet to denounce the Israelites for their sin (6:7-10) and then called Gideon to be a judge.

"When the angel of the LORD appeared to Gideon, he said, 'The Lord is with you, mighty warrior'" (6:12). Surprisingly, Gideon responded with a complaint. "'But sir,' Gideon replied, 'if the LORD is with us, why has all this happened to us? Where are all his wonders that our fathers told us about when they said, "Did not the LORD bring us up out of Egypt?" But now the LORD has abandoned us and put us into the hand of Midian'" (6:13). The Lord didn't bother to deal with Gideon's complaint. "The LORD turned to him and said, 'Go in the strength you have and save Israel out of Midian's hand. Am I not sending you?' 'But LORD,' Gideon asked, 'how can I save Israel? My clan is the weakest in Manasseh, and I am the least in my family.' The LORD answered, 'I will be with you, and you will strike down all the Midianites together'" (6:14-16). Still Gideon was reluctant. He dragged his feet and protested about the Midianite invasion. But his real issue is uncovered in verse 15: "I am the least in my family." I am so small, so unimportant. Don't call me!

The events that followed this dialogue underline Gideon's problem. First, perhaps to convince himself that he wasn't overstepping his spiritual limits, he asked for—and received—permission to offer a sacrifice to the Lord. Gideon's offering of goat meat and bread was miraculously consumed by fire on the altar (6:17-24), a miracle that should have convinced Gideon of the Lord's favor. Then God ordered Gideon to tear down his father's altar to the Canaanite god Baal. Though he obeyed, he did so secretly, at night, for fear of arousing the wrath of Baal-worshipers (6:25-32). Finally, Gideon summoned some of the Israelite tribes to gather with him against the Midianites, but before the battle he panicked again. Twice he demanded that God give him a sign of divine favor—a wet fleece in the morning when the surrounding ground was dry, and then a dry fleece in the morning when the ground around it was wet with dew. Gideon's self-doubts led him over and over to demand signs of God's favor, but God's love for Gideon was so strong and his call so insistent that he granted these signs (6:33-40).

Time and again, Gideon tried to squirm out of God's call, sidetracking the Lord with a theological question ("Why has all this happened to us?" [Judg 6:13]) and generally engaging in what psychologists today call "passive-aggression"—saying yes but meaning no, agreeing to do God's will but all the while dragging his feet. Behind it all, Gideon was convinced that he couldn't do what God commanded him to do: "I am so small. I am weak, incompetent, inconsequential. Even my clan is small—the smallest in the whole tribe of Manasseh." Using modern jargon, his self-esteem was so low and his self-image so poor that he couldn't respond wholeheartedly and affirmatively to the call of God. Reading the dialogue in 6:11-16 and the three events that follow, you can almost sense Gideon's desperation. He was terrified that God was thrusting upon him a task that he was completely unqualified to perform. He tried every delaying tactic he could find to put off the moment when he would actually have to obey.

In the film *The Best of Times*, Robin Williams portrays a businessman in Taft, California. Fifteen years before, as a member of the high school football team, he'd bobbled and then dropped a last-second, potentially game-winning pass in the "big game" against Bakersfield High School. Now, a decade and a half later, he's still obsessed with his failure. Over and over he plays the film of that botched pass, watching himself reach out, touch the ball, bobble it for an agonizing moment, then lose it as he slips and falls facedown into mud. This ancient failure dominates his life, coloring everything in it—his marriage, his business life, his relationships with fellow residents of Taft.

Whenever I see this movie, to some extent I see myself. We all, I suspect, have an "endless-loop" video player in our heads that runs the tape of our failures over and over and over. Suppose I asked you to take a sheet of paper, draw a vertical line right down the middle to form two columns, and write your "positive" qualities in the left-hand column and your "negative" qualities in the right. Which list would be longer? Perhaps like many Christians, you'd draw up a list that accentuates your inabilities, weaknesses, and incompetence. You might erroneously label your list "Humility."

That's what Henry, a parishioner in a church I once served, might have done. No matter how full or empty the church was—even at a weekday Eucharist, when he was the only one there—he would sit at the very back of the building, as far away from the altar as possible. Finally, I asked him one day why he always sat in the last pew. "Because I'm not worthy to be any closer," he told me, and went on to explain that he had learned even as a child to view himself as unworthy of anything—especially of the love of God. Although he knew Jesus loved him, he didn't dare come too close.

That conversation initiated a series of discussions about worthiness and unworthiness and the grace of God. I reminded Henry of the prayer in the Book of Common Prayer: "We do not presume to come to this thy table, O merciful Lord, trusting in our own righteousness, but in thy manifold and great mercy. We are not worthy so much as to gather up the crumbs under thy table. But thou art the same Lord whose property is always to have mercy." Slowly, so very slowly, Henry began to move forward. Over the course of several years, he inched toward the altar. By the time I moved to another parish, he was regularly sitting in the second or third row. Was he worthy? Probably not. After all, none of us are. But was he loved? Infinitely so, by the living God.

Most of us, in one way or another, have a negative picture of ourselves. That picture may have an origin too complex and distant to understand. It may even contain a bit of truth. But whatever the origin or the accuracy of this picture, its effect is obvious. It prevents us from believing that we're really called and imagining that we could be useful for God's purposes. And though it's tempting to give a shallow answer to this problem— "Go ahead! Feel good about yourself! Affirm yourself!"—we're dealing with something deeper and darker that doesn't respond to affirming words, positive thinking, or cheerful expressions. We need something more.

So did Gideon. When God called him, God had to break through the barrier erected by Gideon's self-image, speaking words that Gideon himself couldn't have spoken. "The Lord is with you, mighty warrior" (Judg 6:12). Mighty warrior? The idea would have sounded ridiculous had it come from the lips of Gideon. "Go in the strength you have and save Israel" (6:14). I can almost hear Gideon saying, "You mean I have *strength*, Lord? Strength that would enable me to deliver Israel from the Midianites?"

Of course he did have that strength, but God was the only one who knew it. God was the only one with an absolutely clear picture of Gideon. Yes, God knew that Gideon was the least important member of the smallest clan in Israel. God knew that Gideon would do anything to avoid the task that the Lord was giving him. But God knew something else as well. He looked at Gideon and saw beneath the quaking exterior a mighty warrior, a man of strength. That would not be enough, of course. Before he could lead Israel into battle, "the Spirit of the Lord came upon Gideon" (6:34). His human strength needed divine anointing; only then could he cooperate with God's purposes. Paul, commenting on God's call to Abraham, says, "[Abraham] is the father of us all. As it is written, 'I have made you a father of many nations.' He is our father in the sight of God, in whom he believed—the God who gives life to the dead and *calls things that are not as though they were*" (Rom 4:16-17, italics mine). From Abraham and Sarah, childless for so many years and "as good as dead, came descendants as numerous as the stars in the sky and as countless as the sand on the seashore" (Heb 11:12). In the infertile couple God saw the potential of numberless descendants. And likewise, in the diminutive, shrinking Gideon, God saw a mighty warrior, a man of strength. By his words of affirmation, God called this man forth from an unlikely situation.

God calls forth what we are—our unknown selves that only he sees. At a turning point in his ministry, Jesus asked his disciples, "Who do people say the Son of Man is?" The disciples replied with a list of popular misconceptions about Jesus. "Some say John the Baptist; others say Elijah; and still others, Jeremiah or one of the prophets." Then Jesus put them on the spot. "But what about you? Who do you say I am?" (Matt. 16:13-16). In many ways, what God did to Gideon turns this question around. The question is not, Who do you say that Jesus is? Rather, the question is, *Who does Jesus say you are?* The issue of our self-image isn't resolved by building ourselves up or justifying our lives and even our mistakes. It's resolved instead by listening carefully to what God says about us. Jesus sees the real you. Jesus sees the real me. Jesus calls us forth. The same Lord who said, "I am the light of the world" (John 8:12), also declared, "You are the light of the world" (Matt 5:14).

Yes, of course. God knows our sins, flaws, and weaknesses better than we do. "If we claim to be without sin, we deceive ourselves and the truth is not in us" (1 John 1:8). These words are addressed not to people outside the family of God but to a community of Christians. St. Paul is especially revealing in Romans 7, where he describes his own ongoing struggle with sin, saying, "I do not understand what I do. For what I want to do I do not do, but what I hate I do. . . . I have the desire to do what is good, but I cannot carry it out. For what I do is not the good

I want to do; no, the evil I do not want to do—this I keep on doing" (Rom 7:15, 18-19). When we think of ourselves as spiritually unfit to answer God's call, we are probably right, and God knows it. But even this reality has a healing response from the Lord. As John tells us: "If we confess our sins, he is faithful and just and will forgive us our sins and purify us from all unrighteousness. . . . We have one who speaks to the Father in our defense—Jesus Christ, the Righteous One. He is the atoning sacrifice for our sins" (1 John 1:9; 2:1-2). And Paul, immediately following the spiritual agony he describes in Romans 7, says: "Therefore, there is no condemnation for those who are in Christ Jesus" (Rom 8:1).

The sculptor Michelangelo could look at a block of stone and see in his mind's eye the statue that would emerge from it. He would look at a block—and see *David*. He would look at a block—and see *The Pieta*. When God fixes his gaze upon us, he does the same thing.

That's what he did with Laura, for example, one of the most troubled youths in my parish. She ran away from home constantly, became entangled in the drug culture, and spent time in and out of psychiatric hospitals. By the time she was fifteen, she had run away for good, it seemed; she was among the countless teenage missing persons. Her parents had written her off, and to tell the truth, so had I.

Some eight years passed; I was in a different parish, but Laura tracked me down, called me, and asked for a meeting. I was surprised to hear from her at all, but even more surprised as she told me her story. When she had run away from home that last time, her life continued to plunge deeper and deeper into drugs, deeper and deeper into crime and prostitution to support the drugs. Eventually she was convicted of burglary and sent to a state penitentiary. It was there she met a prison chaplain who could see her not only for what she was but for what she could become. Through this man's ministry, Laura committed her life to Jesus Christ and made some basic decisions about how she would live. By the time she visited me, she was engaged to be married, working as an aide in a substance-abuse rehabilitation facility, and enrolled in college. Eight years before, when I had looked at Laura, I had seen a loser, a lost cause, a "goner." Jesus saw someone very different—a beloved child of God. That prison chaplain was able to look at Laura through the eyes of Jesus and to call forth the person she was meant to be.

How do we deal with our self-image, whatever it may be? We can pray for the ability to see ourselves as Jesus sees us. It is Jesus who knows us best, Jesus who knows the "real you" and the "real me." He knows our sins and weaknesses, yes; but he also knows what we'll look like when we've been "renewed in knowledge in the image of [our] Creator" (Col 3:10).

Questions for Discussion

1.   What experiences have helped to form your own self-image? Has the effect been positive or negative? What impact has your self-image had on your ability to respond to God's call?

2.   "I am the least in my family," said Gideon. How would you define yourself? And how do you imagine God defines you?

3.   What steps do you need to take to change your self-image? How can you overcome the barrier that your self-image erects between yourself and the ministry that God has in mind for you?

4.   Gideon ultimately, and to his own surprise, became the "mighty warrior" whom the Lord called forth. What is God calling forth in you?

-8-

CALLED BY GOD, CALLED BY A MENTOR: SAMUEL

1 Samuel 3:1-18

"SOME PIG!" Charlotte the spider wove into her web this message of hope to protect her friend Wilbur the pig.[1] I wish messages from God were as clear-cut as those in Charlotte's web. A book on God's call starts with the assumption that God actually wants to communicate his will to men and women. But *how* does he do that? Most of us have never heard the voice of God. We have never had the kind of encounter with the Lord that Moses experienced on Mount Sinai or Saul had on the road to Damascus. When God's call comes to us, it's subtle and fleeting: a tug at the heart, a phrase or a sentence from the Bible that seems to jump out of the page, a moment in prayer when we sense that God is giving us—what? A word? A prompting? How can we be sure that what we think is God's call is really God's call? As we saw in chapter 6, his voice often comes to us in hidden, perplexing ways.

This was certainly the case with Samuel. He was the last of the judges (1 Sam 7:15), but his ministry involved much more: He was a prophet (3:19-21) and, most importantly, he was the one who presided over Israel's transition from a loose confederacy ruled by judges to a centralized monarchy (10:1, 23-24; 16:13). Yet when God called him, he neither expected nor recognized the divine voice, but something happened that transformed him and "opened his ears." Like Deborah, Samuel was enabled in the end to hear God's call through another person—not through a whole community as had happened with Deborah but rather through his friend and mentor, Eli. Above all, Samuel's experience tells us that we rarely discern God's call alone.

Toward the end of the time of the judges described in the last chapter of Judges, the principal place of worship for the Israelites was Shiloh in the hill country of the tribe of Ephraim. There the tabernacle, the portable worship center built by Bezalel and Oholiab and their companions, had found a semipermanent home. Its guardians were Eli the priest and his two sons, Hophni and Phinehas. The Israelites made yearly pilgrimage to Shiloh to offer worship and sacrifice to the Lord, and among the pilgrims were a man named Elkanah and his two wives, Hannah and Peninnah. Sadly, Hannah had borne no children (1 Sam 1:1-3). One year, after the sacrifices had been offered, Hannah stood before the Lord. "In bitterness of soul Hannah wept much and prayed to the LORD. And she made a vow, saying, 'O LORD Almighty, if you will only look upon your servant's misery and remember me, and not forget your servant but give her a son, then I will give him to the LORD for all the days of his life'" (1:10-11). Eli overheard the prayer, and after an initial misunderstanding—he thought Hannah was drunk!—he gave her his blessing. Back home, Hannah finally conceived and gave birth to a son, whom she named Samuel. As she had promised, when the child was weaned she brought him to Eli at Shiloh. "I prayed for this child," she told him, "and the LORD has granted me what I asked of him. So now I give him to the LORD. For his whole life he will be given over to the LORD" (1:27-28). And so Samuel became Eli's apprentice at the tabernacle.

Eli's two sons, however, were not made of the same spiritual material as their father. They were guilty of two sins in particular: They expropriated some of the meat that the Israelites intended to offer in sacrifice (2:17), and "they slept with the women who served at the entrance to the Tent of Meeting" (2:22). The spectacle of religious leaders abusing their power is no new phenomenon. Eli, unfortunately, was unable or unwilling to discipline his sons. It was in the midst of this spiritual turmoil that the young Samuel received his call.

"The boy Samuel ministered before the LORD under Eli. In those days the word of the LORD was rare; there were not many visions" (3:1). With these words the story of Samuel's call begins. But we should not pass over them too quickly. They tell us that something was very wrong in Israel, for the Lord had become silent. Why? Perhaps God's silence was connected to the immorality among Israel's religious leaders. Centuries later, the prophet Amos would hear God saying precisely that. "The time is surely coming, says the LORD God, when I will send a famine on the land; not a famine of bread, or a thirst for water, but of hearing the words of the LORD. They shall wander from sea to sea, and from north to east; they shall run to and fro, seeking the word of the LORD, but they shall not find it" (Amos 8:11-12 NRSV). Rebellion against God interrupts communication with him—in both directions. The sins of Hophni and Phinehas were not committed in a vacuum. Israel had been in rebellion over and over during the period of the judges, as we saw in the last chapter. Perpetually hardened hearts had created perpetually deaf ears: "The word of the LORD was rare."

Samuel served in the tabernacle when the spiritual climate of Israel virtually prevented God's word from being heard or received, erecting an additional barrier: *low expectancy*. It had been such a long time since God had spoken that no one expected him to speak! Indeed, God's voice would be so unfamiliar that people wouldn't recognize it even if they heard it. Samuel didn't. He mistook God's voice for Eli's.

Sadly, ancient Israel's spiritual deafness is mirrored by our own. We don't expect to hear God's voice either, and if we did, we might well not recognize it. When I began the steps toward ordination in the Episcopal Church, the application process included a psychiatric exam with a number of accompanying tests. One of them, I recall, asked a series of overlapping questions centering on the issue of "voices": Does God speak to you? Have you ever heard the voice of God? Do you believe God singles you out to talk with you? I found out later that these questions were designed to diagnose schizophrenia. Even in the church we have a cultural barrier that makes us wary of the notion that God might want to communicate his will and purpose to people, not only in a general way but in particular ways for particular individuals. Samuel had no expectation that God would address him personally; nor, often, do we.

"One night Eli, whose eyes were becoming so weak that he could barely see, was lying down in his usual place. The lamp of God had not yet gone out"—it was in the predawn darkness— "and Samuel was lying down in the temple of the LORD, where the ark of God was. Then the LORD called Samuel" (3:2-4). But Samuel didn't recognize him. "He ran to Eli and said, 'Here I am; you called me.' But Eli said, 'I did not call; go back and lie down.' So he went back and lay down" (3:5). But God continued to seek out Samuel. "Again the LORD called, 'Samuel!' And Samuel got up and went to Eli and said, 'Here I am; you called me.' 'My son,' Eli said, 'I did not call; go back and lie down.' Now Samuel did not yet know the LORD: The word of the LORD had not yet been revealed to him" (3:6-7). The boy lacked the spiritual maturity to know who was calling him in the night. He carried out religious duties in the tabernacle, but he had never experienced a personal encounter with the Lord. God was a stranger to him. "The LORD called Samuel a third time, and Samuel got up and went to Eli and said, 'Here I am; you called me.' Then Eli realized that the LORD was calling the boy. So Eli told Samuel, 'Go and lie down, and if he calls you, say, "Speak, LORD, for your servant is listening."' So Samuel went and lay down in his place. The LORD came and stood there, calling as at the other times, 'Samuel! Samuel!' Then Samuel said, 'Speak, for your servant is listening'" (3:8-10). Ironically, the content of God's message included a denunciation of Eli for his failure to curb his sons' immoral activity (3:11-14). Samuel delivered the message to his mentor with reluctance (3:15-17). It speaks well of Eli that he accepted God's verdict with dignity. "Then Eli said, 'He is the LORD; let him do what is good in his eyes'" (3:18).

Two things stand out in God's call to Samuel. *First, Samuel needed help in recognizing God's voice.* Without Eli's discernment Samuel probably never would have realized it was God who called him. The pattern would have gone on endlessly: "Samuel! Samuel!" "Yes, Eli, I'm here."

In recent years, many Christians have rediscovered the ancient concept of "spiritual direction" as Christians enter into an intentional relationship, with one assisting the other in his or her spiritual journey. If I am uncertain about whether it is the Lord who is calling me in a particular area of my life, my spiritual director will help me as a codiscerner. Spiritual directors do not need to be "professionals"; they can be laypersons as well as clergy. The key is that they are growing in their own relationship with the Lord and have gone at least as far as the "directee" in their spiritual journey.

Eli was a classical spiritual director. He listened carefully as Samuel described the late-night voice, and he didn't jump to conclusions. Only after the third encounter was he ready to say, "It is the LORD." Then he told Samuel how to respond to continue the dialogue with God: "Speak, LORD, for your servant is listening." Eli had the maturity and the objectivity to help Samuel hear what the Lord was saying to him. He was an essential person in Samuel's life, someone whose encouragement helped Samuel to listen to God.

I've had an Eli in my own life; his name is Bill. Like Samuel, I went running to Bill when I was faced with a dilemma of my own. In 1977 two parishioners, Ron and Doreen, came to me and dropped a bombshell: "We've received the Holy Spirit!" they said. They had attended something called a Life in the Spirit Seminar in a neighboring parish, a seven-week "crash course" in the Holy

Spirit. The result, they reported, was a newfound joy in the Lord, a deeper sense of his presence, and a profound spiritual renewal. What's more, they recruited twenty of my parishioners to attend the next seminar, just a few weeks ahead. My stomach twisted. I began to imagine my parish filled with wild-eyed Pentecostals, our dignified Anglican worship disrupted by tongues-speaking and other bizarre phenomena, the congregation split into pro- and anti-charismatic factions. What was I to do?

Later that day, I paced in a field behind the church building, stewing over my dilemma. I walked back and forth, back and forth, playing increasingly gruesome scenarios on the motion-picture screen of my mind. Suddenly two words formed themselves. I can't say that I heard a "voice," because there was nothing audible. But there were two words inside my head: *You go.* What? *You go.* I knew exactly what those words meant. I was supposed to attend the Life in the Spirit Seminar myself.

Oh, really? Was this a word from God? Finally, I called my friend Bill, a seminary classmate, and shared the dilemma with him. Bill listened quietly, then said, "Go to the seminar, and God will show you what to do." That was all. Bill's advice was neither deep nor sophisticated. But it turned out that he was my Eli. Over the next few weeks I made a discovery about myself. In Chapter 5 I alluded to an extended "dry" time in my life—not so much a crisis of faith as a crisis of the heart. As I sat at the seminar and listened to a series of fairly basic teachings about the Spirit's work in believers, I saw clearly that I too was needy: thirsty, joyless, obeying the Lord more out of duty than desire. I had become, in the worst sense of the phrase, professionally religious. One night toward the end of the seminar, those twenty parishioners gathered around me and prayed for me: a humbling moment, yes, but one that transformed my life. "Eli's" simple word had enabled me to hear God's call.

Fax machines, e-mail, cell phones, and pagers can make us perpetually accessible. Our communication with God, however, is not so automatic, but still he speaks to us in many ways. Sometimes he speaks softly, in a "gentle whisper" (1 Kgs 19:12). Sometimes he thunders "like the roar of rushing waters" (Ezek 43:2). Sometimes all he seems to do is highlight a word or phrase from the Bible, and we sense that the word is meant specifically for us today. Sometimes an offhand comment from a friend becomes the channel for God's call. Sometimes we simply experience an inner "tug," quiet yet insistent. However God chooses to call us, we need an Eli, a codiscerner, someone who can listen and pray with us.

A second element in Samuel's call stands out: *Samuel had to decide to listen and yield himself to God.* "Speak, LORD, for your servant is listening." Hearing God's call is never passive. It involves two decisions: first, to listen actively for God's word to us; and second, to obey him, whatever he asks. Samuel had to cooperate in a conscious way, opening his heart and presenting his will to the Lord.

More than a thousand years later, Jesus would state this principle in the midst of a discussion with Jewish religious authorities. They were concerned about the source of Jesus' teachings. Where did Jesus get all this learning? "Anyone who resolves to do the will of God," Jesus said, "will know whether the teaching is from God or whether I am speaking on my own" (John 7:17 NRSV). In other words, God will reveal the truth only to those who have decided in advance to obey him, whatever that truth turns out to be. If you approach the Lord tentatively— "Lord, show me your will, and then I'll decide whether to obey"—you'll never discover what his will is. But if you commit yourself beforehand to obedience, God's call will ultimately come with clarity.

Imagine a Christian businessperson, a junior executive named Ted. His company offers him a new position in a distant city that comes with higher stress as well as a higher salary. Should he take the job? If Ted is serious about his commitment to Christ, he might say the following to himself: "Let's see. As I make my decision, I need to consider these factors: the cost of living in the new city, the tax implications of my salary increase, the quality of the schools, the will of God, the perks of the new job, the climate, the stress level I'd have to contend with, the accessibility of good fishing streams." The problem here is that Ted will not learn what the will of God is until he decides in advance to submit himself to it. The "will of God" is not simply one factor among many for a Christian. It is the only factor, the element that controls all others.

Writing a letter of encouragement to the exiles in Babylon, the prophet Jeremiah sent them this word from the Lord: "You will seek me and find me *when you seek me with all your heart. I will be found by you* . . . and will bring you back from captivity" (Jer 29:13-14, italics mine). Finding God contains a proviso. It is not unconditional. Even with the help of an Eli, we must decide to obey.

I cannot turn away from the call of Samuel and the ministry of Eli without posing two questions. *First, who is your "Eli"?* It might be a Christian friend, your spouse, a pastor or other Christian leader, even at times a casual acquaintance. But I believe that God has placed in all of our lives at least one other person—and often many—who can listen and pray and help us to discern the call of God. *Second,who is your "Samuel"?* God has placed us in the lives of our brothers and sisters so that we can provide that word of encouragement that will enable them to say Yes to God's call.

---

[1] See E.B. White, *Charlotte's Web* (New York: Harper and Row, 1952), 77–80.

Questions for Discussion

1.   Samuel lived at a time when "the word of the LORD was rare." How does that compare to our own time? How do people discern God's voice today? How do you?

2.   In a general way, sin and low expectations made it difficult for people to hear God in Samuel's day. What makes it difficult for us?

3.   Eli was something of a spiritual director for Samuel. Who fulfills the role of spiritual director in your life? If there is no one, can you think of a person who might do so?

4.   When you face a major turning point in your life, what drives your decision making? How does seeking God's will relate to the many factors with which you struggle?

-9-

An Unlikely Call: David

1 Samuel 16:1-13

Although Jane and I were to become good friends, her first glimpse of me wasn't very flattering. It was my first Sunday as vicar of St. Joseph's Episcopal Church in Buena Park, California. The congregation had been waiting for months for their new priest, so the church was packed. Everyone was there: regular parishioners, fringe members, friends and relatives of fringe members, people who hadn't been in church since the former vicar had retired. Jane later told me that when the opening hymn ended, she looked up to the front of the church and saw someone she didn't recognize, someone young and scared and out of place. The first words that came into her mind were apparently, *I wonder who the new altar boy is.*

Then she realized, to her horror, that he was the new priest.

We all carry pictures in our minds of what leaders are supposed to look like. Whether the leaders are kings, presidents, teachers, high school principals, den mothers, or pastors, our expectations color the way we look at them. In the sixth grade, for example, my teacher was Mrs. Seifert. She was middle-aged, with laughing eyes and endless stories, always understanding, never critical—in other words, the perfect teacher. Ever since, I have measured teachers by her standard. When my children were in elementary school and I would attend "Back-to-School Night," I found that I held their teachers up against the model, Mrs. Seifert; and, of course, they couldn't measure up. So it was that Samuel—whom we met in the last chapter as a boy—could scarcely believe that God had called David to be the new king. After all, David didn't even *look* like a king!

Somewhat against his will, Samuel had presided over the coronation of Israel's first king, Saul. "The elders of Israel gathered together and came to Samuel at Ramah. They said to him, 'You are old, and your sons do not walk in your ways; now appoint a king to lead us, such as all the other nations have'" (1 Sam 8:4-5). Samuel initially resisted the suggestion. A king, he said, would eventually turn into a tyrant. But when the Israelites' pleas continued, the Lord told him, "Listen to them and give them a king" (8:22). 1 Samuel 9-10 describes the dramatic events surrounding the choice of Saul as king.

But Saul at least looked like a king. "As [Saul] stood among the people he was a head taller than any of the others. Samuel said to all the people, 'Do you see the man the LORD has chosen? There is no one like him among all the people'" (10:23-24). Saul was kingly, in the same sense that we might say a political candidate is presidential. There was something in Saul's bearing and size that appealed to ordinary men and women. He was a man to look up to, figuratively as well as literally. Plus, he had enormous gifts as a military leader. "After Saul had assumed rule over Israel, he fought against their enemies on every side: Moab, the Ammonites, Edom, the kings of Zobah, and the Philistines. Wherever he turned, he inflicted punishment on them" (14:47). In a day when the very existence of God's people was in jeopardy, Saul's military prowess was essential. Finally, Saul generated tremendous personal loyalty. After his first successful military campaign (11:1-11), his leadership was reaffirmed. "The people then said to Samuel, 'Who was it that asked, "Shall Saul reign over us?" Bring these men to us and we will put them to death.' But Saul said, 'No one shall be put to death today, for this day the LORD has rescued Israel'" (11:12-13). Saul seemed to have the instinctive political skills to maintain a high level of support among the people.

Unfortunately, Saul's kingship ended in failure. Early in his reign, he showed a tendency to rebel against the Lord, and this ultimately led to his downfall. At one point, for example, rather than waiting for the arrival of Samuel, Saul impatiently offered a sacrifice to the Lord—a practice that required a priest. When Samuel arrived, he stormed at Saul, "What have you done? . . . You acted foolishly. . . . You have not kept the command the LORD your God gave you; if you had, he would have established your kingdom over Israel for all time. But now your kingdom will not endure" (13:11, 13-14). Later, God ordered Saul to exterminate the wicked Amalekites and all their possessions. "But Saul and the army spared Agag [the Amalekite king] and the best of the sheep and cattle, the fat calves and lambs—everything that was good" (15:9). God's reaction was immediate. "I am grieved," he told Samuel, "that I have made Saul king" (15:10); and Samuel said to Saul, "Rebellion is like the sin of divination, and arrogance like the evil of idolatry. Because you have rejected the word of the LORD, he has rejected you as king" (15:23). The stage was set for a new king.

"The LORD said to Samuel, 'How long will you mourn for Saul, since I have rejected him as king over Israel? Fill your horn with oil and be on your way; I am sending you to Jesse of Bethlehem. I have chosen one of his sons to be king'" (16:1). When Samuel arrived in Bethlehem, he asked Jesse and his sons to present themselves. "When they came, he looked on Eliab and thought, 'Surely the LORD's anointed is now before the LORD.' But the LORD said to Samuel, 'Do not look on his appearance or on the height of his stature, because I have rejected him; for the LORD does not see as mortals see; they look on the outward appearance, but the LORD looks on the heart'" (16:6-7 NRSV). Inevitably, Samuel's mental picture of a king was shaped by Saul. With all of his flaws, Saul was a strong and self-assured leader, so Samuel had clear expectations about what a king should look like. Eliab seemed to be the one, but God had someone else in mind.

"Then Jesse called Abinadab and had him pass in front of

Samuel. But Samuel said, 'The LORD has not chosen this one either.' Jesse then had Shammah pass by, but Samuel said, 'Nor has the LORD chosen this one.' Jesse had seven of his sons pass before Samuel, but Samuel said to him, 'The LORD has not chosen these'" (16:8-10). God had ordered Samuel to choose a new king from among Jesse's sons; some of them at least *looked* appropriate, but the Lord vetoed them all.

"So [Samuel] asked Jesse, 'Are these all the sons you have?' 'There is still the youngest,' Jesse answered, 'but he is tending the sheep.' Samuel said, 'Send for him; we will not sit down until he arrives'" (16:11). This eighth and youngest son was so unimportant that Jesse hadn't thought to invite him to the sacrifice. "So [Jesse] sent and had him brought in. He was ruddy, with a fine appearance and handsome features. Then the LORD said, 'Rise and anoint him; he is the one'" (16:12). In a society where the firstborn son automatically had priority, where leadership depended on size, military prowess, and personal charisma, this youngest son was an unlikely choice. He was the last-born, the smallest, and the one given menial tasks while his elder brothers tended to more important business.

We know the rest of the story. We know about Goliath, about the military victories, about his succeeding Saul as king. We know that David became the ideal king, against whom all other kings in Israel were measured (see 1 Kgs 15:1-5, 9-11). We know that the New Testament carefully traces Jesus' ancestry to David (Matt 1:1, 6, 16; Luke 3:31-32) and assigns to Jesus the title "Son of David" (Mark 10:47-48; see also Rom 1:3). We know too about David's sins and failures: his adulterous relationship with Bathsheba and murder of her husband (1 Sam 11:1-27) and his inability to control his children (13:1-22). Even his weaknesses seem larger than life. But Samuel had no crystal ball. He knew none of this. He looked at David: the youngest, the smallest, the least kingly. He was handsome, yes—but that's hardly a qualification for leadership in an age when strength and size were essential. Yet God said to Samuel, "Rise and anoint him; he is the one." Those may have been the most shocking words Samuel had ever heard.

"So Samuel took the horn of oil and anointed him in the presence of his brothers, and from that day on the Spirit of the Lord came upon David in power" (16:13). Anointing with oil was the usual way that leaders were set apart in ancient Israel (1 Sam 10:1; 1 Kgs 1:38-40, 19:15-16; 2 Kgs 9:1-3). Even the title we give to Jesus—Christ—simply translates the Hebrew word "Messiah," which means the anointed one: Jesus has been anointed "with the Holy Spirit and power" (Acts 10:38) to be the King of kings, our Lord and Savior. What is unusual about David's anointing is that 1 Samuel stresses that the Spirit permanently dwelt in David from that moment on. Throughout the Old Testament, the Holy Spirit was given to select individuals as a kind of temporary empowerment (Judg 6:34; 14:6, 19), but the prophet Joel looked forward to the day when the Holy Spirit would be given to all people (Joel 2:28-32), a prophecy not fulfilled until Pentecost (Acts 2:1-4, 14-21). David stands alone among Old Testament figures as a Spirit-filled person in whom the Holy Spirit permanently dwelt.

The unlikely call of David tells us three things about God's dealings with humankind in general and us in particular. *First, at turning points in his plan of redemption, God often issues an unlikely call.* Abraham was a homeless nomad who left the security of civilization for the uncertainty of life in a tent. Jacob was a scoundrel and a liar, hardly the model of a godly man. Moses was an exile from his home in Egypt, separated from both the people of his birth and the royalty among whom he'd been raised. Over and over, as God's plan to rescue men and women from sin and death moved forward, God chose someone totally unpredictable: Gideon, Amos, even Cyrus the Persian, a pagan monarch. The New Testament is filled with unlikely selections too—not only the Twelve, but also Saul the Pharisee who became

Paul the Apostle, and Mary Magdalene, first to proclaim Jesus' resurrection. Throughout the history of the Christian Church, God has continued to single out the most unlikely people to bring renewal and the challenge of a deeper commitment to Jesus Christ. There was Augustine of Hippo, who experimented with a multitude of philosophies and immoral lifestyles before surrendering to the Lord. There was Francis of Assisi, a medieval "flower child" whose simplicity and poverty confronted a church grown rich and stagnant. There was Martin Luther, an emotional and unstable monk, searching for peace and discovering it in the neglected truth that we are "justified by faith in Christ and not by observing the law" (Gal 2:16).

The most unlikely call of all, of course, came in the life around which all of human history revolves: the call of Jesus Christ. The King of kings, he was born not in luxury but in a stable. He is the one at whose name "every knee should bow, in heaven and on earth and under the earth" (Phil 2:10), yet for most of his earthly life his sphere of operation was not a center of power like Rome or Jerusalem, but lowly Nazareth. "He is before all things, and in him all things hold together. And he is the head of the body, the church; he is the beginning and the firstborn from among the dead, so that in everything he might have the supremacy" (Col 1:17-18). Yet he died not the glorious death of a soldier but the ignominious death of a criminal. Nothing about him from the human point of view separated him from his brothers and sisters.

Second, God's people often have a hard time recognizing the unlikely one whom God has called. This was certainly the case with our Lord. "He came to what was his own, and his own people did not accept him" (John 1:11 NRSV). Consistently people failed to discern his uniqueness. Neither his family (Mark 3:20-21) nor his disciples (John 14:9) fully comprehended who he was and what he had come to do. He did not look like the Messiah whom the Jews were expecting. He was not a warrior or

a political leader or a member of the religious establishment. He
fit into no predetermined mold. Among his people he moved as
a stranger.

We too have a difficult time recognizing God's call, in
ourselves or others. We carry around unspoken expectations,
never acknowledged, that affect the way we see people and the
way we see ourselves. These expectations may be physical, having
to do with age or size or bearing. They may be social, having to
do with culture or race or educational level. They may even be
spiritual: We may look for God to select people who belong to
our denomination, who use our particular Christian "lingo,"
who project the kind of image that conforms to our picture of
holiness.

Years ago a parishioner asked me to visit his father,
Howard, and to bring him Holy Communion. Howard was a
relatively young man, in his late 50s, but he suffered from a
severe heart problem that involved both valves and arteries. He
was too weak for surgery, yet he couldn't survive without it.
When I walked into Howard's room for the first time, I was
overwhelmed by his collection of religious bric-a-brac: statues,
icons, candles, plaques of the Sacred Heart, crucifixes, holy cards,
a bottle of holy water, rosaries dangling from doorknobs.
Episcopalians are supposed to be tolerant, but I confess that
some repressed anti-Roman Catholic bigotry bubbled to the
surface. I said nothing, of course, just went on with a routine
visit. But in my heart I didn't take Howard seriously. The room
and its contents symbolized to me the worst kind of skin-deep
spirituality. As efficiently as I could, I gave Howard the sacrament, packed up my Communion set, and prepared to take my
leave. Howard looked up at me and said, "You know, Father Ed,
if I don't make it through this illness, I'll be okay. I know that I'm
going to heaven, because Jesus is living in my heart." Suddenly
my preconceptions crashed around me. I discovered that
Howard, despite my callous, silent dismissal, was among the

beloved and chosen of the Lord.

Third, remember that we are all the recipients of an unlikely call. St. Paul was certainly aware of this reality. Constantly in his letters he reminds his readers and himself that he had a checkered spiritual past. "I thank Christ Jesus our Lord, who has given me strength, that he considered me faithful, appointing me to his service. Even though I was once a blasphemer and a persecutor and a violent man, I was shown mercy because I acted in ignorance and unbelief. . . . Christ Jesus came into the world to save sinners—of whom I am the worst" (1 Tim 1:12-13, 15; cf. 1 Cor 15:8-9; Gal 1:13, 23; Phil 3:6). His Letter to the Romans is an extended introduction of himself to a congregation he had not yet met. Yet even here he alluded to the unlikeliness of his call. "Through [Jesus] and for his name's sake, we received grace and apostleship to call people from among all the Gentiles to the obedience that comes from faith" (Rom 1:5). Grace, the free gift of God's love to undeserving sinners, is linked to apostleship. He couldn't have had one without the other.

Our call to believe in and follow Jesus Christ, to be filled with his Spirit, to belong to his family the Church, to serve him in ministries as close as our own homes and as far away as the other side of the planet—all of that is a gift. Yes, we know that we have flaws, character defects, weaknesses. If I imagine God scanning the face of the earth looking for a new disciple for his Son, I would never expect him to call *me*. I might not expect him to call you, either. None of us is a likely choice. David certainly wasn't. On a human level, God should have picked Eliab! "I the LORD search the heart and examine the mind" (Jer 17:10); and so, beyond our expectations, he chooses us to be friends of Jesus and citizens of his kingdom (2 Cor 5:20).

Questions for Discussion

1. Jesse simply assumed that his son David was "out of the running" as Samuel sought a king. What expectations, deliberately chosen or accidental, inform your ability to identify God's call in others? In yourself?

2. Can you think of a Christian who, in your experience, was an unlikely candidate for God's call—and yet has been used powerfully for God's purposes? How has that person affected your life?

3. What do you need to do to overcome your own preconceptions concerning "suitable" candidates for God's call?

4. In what ways are you an unlikely recipient of God's call? How has God called you despite this?

-10-

CALL FORWARDING: ELIJAH AND ELISHA

1 Kings 19:1-21; 2 Kings 2:1-15

On Fifth Avenue near Rockefeller Center, Atlas holds up the world. As a teenager growing up in New York City, I walked past the statue almost daily, and I often marveled at how cruel the ancient Greek myth was. The gods doomed one man to carry the weight of the world on his shoulders forever—no relief, no time-outs, just the terrible burden that went on and on and on.

We too carry burdens that seem to go on and on and on: the burden of our families, the burden of our jobs or our school-work, the burden of trying to live a life consistent with our Christian commitment, the burden of paying the bills or taking care of a chronically ill parent or struggling with a permanently rebellious or sick child. We resonate with the Church of our Lady of Perpetual Responsibility in Garrison Keillor's Lake Wobegon stories. We live with a need to do our duty, to get things done, to perform. Yet we also live daily with the desire, if we dare admit it, to get out from under the burden. But how?

The prophet Elijah discovered that part of God's call to him was the call to relinquish his call. He discovered that God didn't intend that he carry the burden forever. In many ways, the most important thing Elijah ever did was to commission a successor.

After King David's long and prosperous reign, the Israelites suffered under a series of increasingly dysfunctional monarchs. Solomon, a thoroughly "mixed" character, combined wisdom (1 Kgs 3:4-28) and devotion (8:14-61) with administrative tyranny (9:15-23) and religious syncretism (11:1-6), the tenden-cy to blend worship of the one true God with devotions import-ed from paganism. His son Rehoboam so alienated the Israelites that eventually the kingdom was divided into two realms, Judah in the south and Israel in the north (12:1-17). A series of corrupt dynasties in the north culminated in the reign of Ahab (874-853 B.C.E.). "[Ahab] married Jezebel daughter of Ethbaal king of the Sidonians, and began to serve Baal and worship him. He set up an altar for Baal in the temple of Baal that he built in Samaria [the capital of the northern kingdom]" (16:31-32). This set the stage for conflict between Ahab and his nemesis, the prophet Elijah.

"When [Ahab] saw Elijah, he said to him, 'Is that you, you troubler of Israel?' 'I have not made trouble for Israel,' Elijah replied. 'But you and your father's family have. You have abandoned the LORD's commands and have followed the Baals'" (1 Kgs 18:17-18). Elijah demanded that Ahab gather the prophets of Baal on Mount Carmel for a face-off: The prophets were to set up an altar to Baal, sacrifice a bull on it, and call on their god to answer by fire; Elijah would do the same with the Lord. The results would show which deity was truly divine. The prophets of Baal failed to arouse their god, and "at noon Elijah began to taunt them. 'Shout louder!' he said. 'Surely he is a god! Perhaps he is deep in thought, or busy, or traveling. Maybe he is sleeping and must be awakened'" (18:27). When Elijah presented his offering to the Lord, "the fire of the LORD fell and burned up the sacrifice, the wood, the stones and the soil, and also licked up the water in the trench. When all the people saw this, they fell prostrate and cried, 'The LORD—he is God! The LORD—he is God!'" (18:38-39). Elijah ordered the crowd to kill the 450 prophets of Baal, an order they quickly obeyed; as a sign of the Lord's favor, a drought that had lasted more than three years was broken that same day (18:40-46). This should have been a time of great rejoicing for Elijah.

Instead, Elijah sank into depression. Queen Jezebel, furious at what had happened to her prophets, sent a threat to Elijah: "May the gods deal with me, be it ever so severely, if by this time tomorrow I do not make your life like that of one of them" (19:2). Elijah had just fearlessly challenged the king and all of those prophets, but when Jezebel threatened, he panicked. He fled south into the Judean desert and "prayed that he might die. 'I have had enough, LORD,' he said. 'Take my life'" (19:4). An angel of the Lord provided miraculous food, on the strength of which Elijah "traveled forty days and forty nights until he reached Horeb, the mountain of God" (19:8). An exhausted and frightened Elijah spent the night in a cave there, and God asked, "What are you doing here, Elijah?" (19:9). In his answer, and in Elijah's interactions with God that follow, God says three things to Elijah about his long-carried, terrible burden of being the Lord's prophet through fierce and ongoing opposition.

First, you are not alone. Elijah believed that he and he alone had been faithful to the Lord. "I have been very zealous for the LORD God Almighty," he said. "The Israelites have rejected your covenant, broken down your altars, and put your prophets to death with the sword. I am the only one left, and now they are trying to kill me too" (19:10). He felt isolated not only from the Israelite rulers who had been worshiping false gods but also from his entire nation. No one understood. No one was faithful. He was fighting a lonely battle for the Lord, and his sense of separation had finally caught up with him. His complaint that he was "the only one left" has the feel of self-pity about it, but it's an emotion we can understand. Like the policeman Javert in Hugo's *Les Miserables*, Elijah saw himself as the sole agent of righteousness, and the result was a profound and destructive loneliness.

God responded to Elijah's sense of isolation with an epiphany—a manifestation of his power—and a word. First, God ordered Elijah to stand on the mountain while he passed by. Divine pyrotechnics followed: a tremendous wind, an earthquake, fire. But the Lord was in none of these. "And after the fire came a gentle whisper [NRSV, "a sound of sheer silence"]. When Elijah heard it, he pulled his cloak over his face and went out and stood at the mouth of the cave" (1 Kgs 19:12-13). God's presence, however, didn't cure Elijah's loneliness. God repeated his question: "What are you doing here, Elijah?" Elijah responded precisely as before: "I have been very zealous. . . . I am the only one left" (19:13-14). So the Lord had a word for him. "Go back the way you came, and go to the Desert of Damascus. When you get there, anoint Hazael king over Aram. Also, anoint Jehu son of Nimshi king over Israel, and anoint Elisha son of Shaphat from Abel Meholah to succeed you as prophet. . . . *Yet I reserve seven thousand in Israel*—all whose knees have not bowed down to Baal and all whose mouths have not kissed him" (19:15-16, 18, italics mine). You are not alone, God was saying. I am giving you allies and even a prophet to follow you. Above all, God told Elijah, you must know that there are seven thousand faithful people in Israel. Elijah's isolation was in part self-imposed, the result of a spiritual blindness that kept him from seeing the many who hadn't followed Ahab and Jezebel into the worship of Baal.

You may need to hear the same message. You may be the only follower of Jesus in your family or household, and experience the isolating sense that no one knows or loves the Person at the center of your life. Or you may feel isolated in the work-place—perhaps pressured to speak or act in a way inconsistent with your calling as a believer. Or perhaps you simply have nothing in common with your fellow workers. The body of Christ itself, God's own family, can be a lonely place; theological controversy or a diversity of vision can separate us from brothers and sisters. Your response in all of these situations may be the same as Elijah's: "I am the only one left." So God reminds you: You are not alone.

I have learned this truth, surprisingly, at funerals. Clergy are often asked to conduct services for people who were not (and may never have been) members of the church. In that kind of setting, I have to trust that the Lord will make the Scriptures and the prayers and the sermon take on new life in Christ and use it all to his glory in the lives of the mourners. But this kind of funeral is a dry and very lonely experience. My words seem to float off into the room, and I cannot tell if anyone is hearing them, if what I am saying makes any difference or even any sense to them. But in these situations, I've come to expect a gift: *Always* at this type of funeral God sends at least one Christian. During the sermon I spot the person; he or she is nodding or smiling or in some way offering a ministry of nonverbal encouragement. My fellow Christian is a reminder from the Lord in the midst of a service otherwise dry and lonely that I am not alone.

Second, you are replaceable. This was a word that Elijah very much needed to hear. He had fallen into the trap of believing that he was so indispensable to God that he could never stop, not for a moment. He was, he thought, the only one left, and so God's plan depended on him alone. When the Lord commanded him to "anoint Elisha son of Shaphat from Abel Meholah to succeed you" (1 Kgs 19:16), I suspect he felt a sense of relief. You are not as essential as you think, God was telling him. You can be replaced. You *will* be replaced. "So Elijah went from there and found Elisha son of Shaphat. He was plowing with twelve yoke of oxen, and he himself was driving the twelfth pair. Elijah went up to him and threw his cloak around him" (19:19). After Elisha had said good-bye to his relatives and symbolized his new life by serving his oxen as a meal and using the farm implements for the cooking fire, "he set out to follow Elijah and became his attendant" (19:21). We do not know about the state of Elijah's inner life when his designated successor joined him, but I hope he felt a new freedom. His call wasn't an endless burden. The intolerable pressure had come to an end.

Every Christian needs to hear this message. At times we can feel utterly depleted as we pour ourselves out until we have nothing left to give, convinced that we're completely irreplaceable and that no one can do what we do. This crushing sense of our indispensability can afflict any Christian, whether the cause of the burden is in our family life, in our work or school, in community involvement, or in our commitment to the institutional church. We need to know that we *are* replaceable; that every ministry and every call—except our call to belong to Jesus—will come to an end, and not just with our death. Many callings will cease when we hand them over to people God has appointed to succeed us. The kingdom of God is built by a succession of saints, one after another, like the links of a chain. No one link is the whole chain. Even the apostle Paul, when he saw his death approaching, prepared his assistant Timothy to succeed him: "Guard the good deposit that was entrusted to you—guard it with the help of the Holy Spirit who lives in us" (2 Tim 1:14). Earlier, Paul had reminded Timothy of his call: "Do not neglect your gift, which was given you through a prophetic message when the body of elders laid their hands on you" (1 Tim 4:14). Paul was replaceable because the Lord had raised up Timothy.

I learned this lesson too in my own parish. Sarah had been a lifelong church member, but it wasn't until her 40s that something in a sermon triggered an internal "Ah ha!" and she committed her life to our Lord in a deliberate and conscious way. In time, she began to take on ministries in the parish. She joined the finance committee, superintended the Sunday school, coordinated weekend seminars, organized prayer and praise services, brought meals to the sick, and ultimately became senior warden. I came to depend on her leadership in virtually every aspect of the church's life.

And then she moved. Her husband received a transfer to Dallas, and the whole family was suddenly gone. I was devastated and frightened. How could we get along without her? We depended on her for so much: ministry after ministry was in her care.

That was when we made a discovery. Sarah was replaceable. As soon as she was gone, people began to step forward spontaneously—there was no time to look for recruits, so quickly did all of those jobs get filled. It turned out that Sarah's very leaving was part of her calling, because it was in the leaving that the Lord raised up a host of Christians willing to serve. We need to know that we can be replaced. Only Jesus is irreplaceable!

Third, you are duplicatable. As Elijah's life and ministry were coming to an end, he traveled to the Jordan River, accompanied by Elisha. At each stop on the way, a company of prophets warned Elisha: "Do you know that the LORD is going to take your master from you today?" (2 Kgs 2:3, 5). Elisha was well aware, and he insisted on being with Elijah until the end. When they arrived at the Jordan, "Elijah took his cloak"—the same cloak he had thrown over Elisha as a symbol of the latter's call—"rolled it up and struck the water with it. The water divided to the right and to the left, and the two of them crossed over on dry ground. When they had crossed, Elijah said to Elisha, 'Tell me, what can I do for you before I am taken from you?' 'Let me inherit a double portion of your spirit,' Elisha replied" (2:8-9). Elisha was not merely being greedy. A "double portion" meant that Elisha was Elijah's proper heir. In this case, Elisha knew that he needed more than a commission to take over Elijah's ministry. He needed the power that had enabled Elijah to confront kings and rulers (1 Kgs 21), provide miraculous food for a starving widow (17:7-16), and even raise the dead (17:17-24). And so Elijah told Elisha, "You have asked a difficult thing, . . . yet if you see me when I am taken from you, it will be yours—otherwise not" (2 Kgs 2:10).

Elisha's request was granted. "Suddenly a chariot of fire and horses of fire appeared and separated the two of them, and Elijah went up to heaven in a whirlwind. Elisha saw this and cried out, 'My father! My father! The chariots and horsemen of Israel!' . . . He picked up the cloak that had fallen from Elijah and went back and stood on the bank of the Jordan. Then he took the cloak that had fallen from him and struck the water with it. 'Where now is the LORD, the God of Elijah?' he asked. When he struck the water, it divided to the right and to the left, and he crossed over. The company of the prophets from Jericho, who were watching, said, 'The spirit of Elijah is resting on Elisha'" (2:11-15). Elisha was enabled to do what Elijah had done. Elijah's ministry was reproduced in the ministry of his apprentice.

The New Testament also tells us that ministry can be duplicated. Jesus spent three years teaching his disciples to do what he did: "Preach this message," he said: "'The kingdom of heaven is near.' Heal the sick, raise the dead, cleanse those who have leprosy, drive out demons" (Matt 10:7-8). Do what I have been doing.

We need more than just marching orders, however; we need the power to carry them out. At the Last Supper, Jesus made promises about this power. "I tell you the truth, anyone who has faith in me will do what I have been doing. He will do even greater things than these, because I am going to the Father" (John 14:12). Greater things? But how? "I tell you the truth: It is for your good that I am going away. Unless I go away, the Counselor will not come to you; but if I go, I will send him to you" (16:7-8).

All of this is both humbling and heartening. It is humbling because it means that God does not *need* us! Whatever our call today, it will pass. God will place it in someone else's care. We are "stewards" (1 Cor 4:1 NRSV), temporary managers of God's affairs, free to say yes and to leave the results in God's hands. Perhaps Elijah experienced some of that same humbling, and that same freedom, as he ascended in the whirlwind.

Elijah's story is heartening as well. If we are dispensable, there is a corollary: Jesus is Lord. Only he is indispensable! He calls us, he empowers us, and then he releases us from our call. The kingdom of God is, in the end, his work, not ours. Every time we pray the Lord's Prayer—"Your kingdom come"—we acknowledge our dependence on the King of kings.

Questions for Discussion

1. "I am the only one left," Elijah said. In what ways do you imagine yourself as indispensable? How does that impact the way you view your ministry?

2. Who are the people God has sent into your life to remind you that you are not alone? How have they supported you in your call?

3. As you consider specific aspects of your call—in the Church, in your home, at work—what is your reaction to the possibility that the Lord may someday (perhaps soon!) replace you? Does this bring joy or a sense of burden? Are there any ministries God may be asking you to relinquish today?

4. How may the Lord be calling you to duplicate your ministry in others, to train them to do what you are doing?

-11-

CALLED IN BROKENNESS: HOSEA

Hosea 1-3

Frederick Buechner's *Godric* tells the story of a twelfth-century English hermit who spent the last 62 years of his life in a hut by the river Wear near Durham. Shortly before his death, a monk named Reginald comes to Godric for help in writing the old hermit's biography. Godric is ill-tempered, sharp, scornful; he cooperates only grudgingly with Reginald. The book nearly completed, Reginald reads portions of it to Godric:

> "His beard was thick," he reads, "and longer than the ordinary, his mouth well-shaped with lips of moderate thickness. In youth his hair was black, in age as white as snow. His neck was short and thick, knotted with veins and sinews. His legs were some-what slender, his instep high, his knees hardened and horny from frequent kneeling. His whole skin was rough beyond the ordinary until all this roughness was softened by old age. Such was the external appearance of this saint."
>
> "This SAINT!" I cry. Then there's a roaring in my ears as if all the blood I have in me is sucked into my head at once with pain so cruel I think my skull will fly apart. Reginald goes pale as death and hastes to me. I push him off. "Blasphemer! Fool!" I cry. Half blind, I try to crawl away, and when he seeks to succor me, I turn and would have bit his hand had he not leaped aside.[1]

Godric, of course, doesn't think of the word "saint" in its New Testament sense, referring to all Christian people. For him, a saint is a holy man, so perfectly transformed into Christ's image that all imperfections, all hints of brokenness, have vanished. No wonder he protests. He's not perfect—far from it. His life is seriously disordered and his flaws dreadfully apparent, not only to Godric himself, but to the whole world.

So are ours. Though we've been born anew (John 3:5), cleansed by the blood of Jesus (1 John 1:7), marked with the gift of the Holy Spirit (Eph 1:13), given the right to be called children of God (John 1:12)—we are still broken people. Like Godric, in our moments of honest self-awareness we see our self-centeredness, our inability to love without conditions, our failure to reflect Jesus in the way we deal with people and possessions and power. More than that, in our self-awareness we see ourselves as part of a world where broken relationships are the norm, where emotional and physical pain are ordinary, where alienation and loneliness can dominate us for a week, a month, even a whole lifetime. So we can rightly wonder: *Am I of any earthly use to the Lord? In my state of brokenness and imperfection, in my sin and pain and woundedness, can I be an agent of the kingdom of God?* The story of Hosea tells us that the answer is yes.

Hosea lived in the mid-700s B.C.E., as the northern kingdom of Israel was in rapid decline. Under Jeroboam II (793-753 B.C.E.), Israel enjoyed a period of peace and prosperity, but in the years that followed, twin threats emerged. First, political instability seemed to overwhelm the nation—in the space of twenty-five years, six kings reigned, four of whom were assassinated, and dynastic chaos led to economic decline. Second, with the accession of Tiglath-Pileser 1 of Assyria in 745 B.C.E., the threat of invasion by the formerly quiet empire of Assyria on Israel's northern border was renewed. These internal and external dangers were balanced by a subtler and in many ways a more destructive threat. Something gnawed at Israel's soul.

When the ten northern tribes separated themselves from Judah, forming Israel in 930 B.C.E., their first king set up shrines at the southern and northern ends of the region to compete with Judah's temple in Jerusalem. At these shrines bogus priests presided over idolatrous religious ceremonies, and in the two centuries that followed, Israel's spiritual decline continued. The Israelites tended to blend worship of the one true God with ceremonies honoring the fertility deities of the Canaanites, seeking to ensure the fruitfulness of the soil by acting out the sexual union of Baal and Ashtoreth, the fertility deities. Worshipers, uniting with temple prostitutes, believed that Baal and Ashtoreth would watch the proceedings, be reminded of their duty, and engage in their own heavenly coupling. This would guarantee fertile soil and excellent harvests.

Many Israelites were attracted to this religion. By the time of Hosea in the mid-700s, Canaanite religion had achieved a prominent place in the northern kingdom's life. No longer were the Israelites "a people holy to the LORD" (Deut 7:6), set apart as worshipers of the God of Abraham, Isaac, and Jacob. On the contrary, they were hardly distinguishable from their pagan neighbors. It was this spiritual devastation that God addressed through the ministry of the prophet Hosea.

The surprising thing about Hosea's ministry is that it emerged not from his strength but from his brokenness. Hosea was involved in a disastrous marriage with a woman named Gomer. But the very pain that Hosea felt at Gomer's unfaithfulness allowed him to see into the heart of God, knowing something of God's pain when Israel rejected him and worshiped Baal and Ashtoreth. Hosea's story, told in the form of narrative and poetry, interweaves God's pain at Israel's unfaithfulness with Hosea's pain at Gomer's. It's a story of love and pain, rejection and reclamation, both the prophet's and the Lord's.

"When the LORD began to speak through Hosea, the LORD said to him, 'Go, take to yourself an adulterous wife and children of unfaithfulness, because the land is guilty of the vilest adultery in departing from the LORD.' So he married Gomer daughter of Diblaim, and she conceived and bore him a son" (Hos 1:2-3). This marriage was no accident, no sudden decision in the bloom of romance. At the very outset, Hosea knew that he was marrying a woman whose moral character was suspect, who—though we're not sure—may even have been a prostitute in the temple of the Canaanite fertility deities. Hosea was well aware of the kind of marriage he was entering.

The prophet and his wife had three children. The first, a son, was named Jezreel, which means "God scatters." A daughter followed. "Then the LORD said to Hosea, 'Call her Lo-Ruhamah [which means "not loved"], for I will no longer show love to the house of Israel, that I should at all forgive them" (1:6). The final child, another boy, was named Lo-Ammi ("not my people"), "for you are not my people, and I am not your God" (1:9). Hosea's three children each carried a name that symbolized some aspect of Israel's broken relationship with God. Even more profoundly, the unraveling of Hosea's marriage to Gomer reveals the depths of God's own pain at Israel's unfaithfulness. Though the details are sketchy, it seems that Gomer left Hosea and entered (or reentered) a life of prostitution. But God sent Hosea after her. "The LORD said to me, 'Go, show your love to your wife again, though she is loved by another and is an adulteress. Love her as the LORD loves the Israelites, though they turn to other gods and love the sacred raisin cakes [used in the worship of Baal]'" (3:1). Hosea apparently went to the pagan temple, found Gomer, and paid money to buy her out of the slavery that shrine prostitution entailed. "So I bought her for fifteen shekels of silver and about a homer and a lethek of barley. Then I told her, 'You are to live with me many days; you must not be a prostitute or be intimate with any man, and I will live with you'" (3:2-3). Hosea was a man who could love, forgive, and reclaim his beloved, despite the pain that Gomer's unfaithfulness brought him. More than that, he "went public" with his pain: no cover-up, no stiff upper lip. Hosea allowed his brokenness to become not only a matter for public consumption but the vehicle that made his prophetic ministry possible.

Hosea's story tells us three things not only about God's love but also about the nature of his call. *First, God may call you before you are ready, while your life is still in turmoil.* Hosea's ministry began while his domestic disaster was in progress. In modern jargon, his family was so dysfunctional that God should have disqualified him. Instead, God called him just as he was entering a time of brokenness, alienation, and pain. God didn't wait for Hosea to get his life in order.

We too are often tempted to look at our lives and see the brokenness that should disqualify us from responding to God's call. Our brokenness might be a painful marriage, or troubles with our children, or difficulty paying the bills. It might concern stress at work—or stress over lack of work. It might involve broken relationships or a broken heart. It might be completely hidden: depression, loneliness, fear. It might be a sin or a compulsive behavior from which, despite our best efforts, we can't get free. We can all identify areas of our lives that are disordered. The question, as I said at the beginning of the chapter, is this: Given the reality of my brokenness, am I of any earthly use to the Lord? My instinctive answer is no. God needs to find someone who has gotten his or her act together, someone who has worked through problems and come out on the other side. I am assuredly not that person!

Years ago I heard a very wise nun named Sister Mariana say that Christians often put off serving God until a time "when things get back to normal." We say, "Lord, I'll serve you when tax season is over . . . when things quiet down at the office . . . when I finally get my kids in line . . . when I don't have such a crowded appointment book . . . when I'm feeling better about myself . . . when I'm making enough money that I don't have to worry all the time . . . when my marriage is healed . . . when my ulcer gets better . . . when I stop drinking . . . when things get back to normal." All of these are significant problems that deserve our attention. Some of them will be healed in this life; some may not—"normal" may never come. But God calls us before we're ready, and he expects us to answer.

Second, the turmoil itself may be part of the call. For Hosea, the pain of his broken marriage is what gave him entry into God's broken heart. He spoke of God's anger and pain, God's love and forgiveness, with an authenticity he otherwise would not have conveyed. His turmoil was not so much a distraction from his call as it was an essential element in it. Henri Nouwen recounts a story from the Talmud about the Messiah:

> Rabbi Yoshua ben Levi came upon Elijah the prophet while he was standing at the entrance of Rabbi Simeon ben Yohai's cave. . . .
> He asked Elijah, "When will the Messiah come?"
> Elijah replied, "Go ask him yourself."
> "Where is he?"
> "Sitting at the gates of the city."
> "How shall I know him?"
> "He is sitting among the poor covered with wounds. The others unbind all their wounds at the same time and then bind them up again. But he unbinds one at a time and binds it up again, saying to himself, 'Perhaps I shall be needed; if so I must always be ready so as not to delay for a moment.'"[2]

Christians believe that the Messiah has come and that he has indeed been wounded on the cross. Nouwen adds, "Like Jesus, he who proclaims liberation is called not only to care for his own wounds and the wounds of others, but also to make his wounds into a major source of healing power"[3] Our very weakness and brokenness can enable us to touch others in Jesus' name.

Jesus himself ministered out of brokenness. "You know the grace of our Lord Jesus Christ, that though he was rich, yet for your sakes he became poor" (2 Cor 8:9). Indeed, it was precisely in the moment of greatest weakness, when "he was pierced for our transgressions, . . . crushed for our iniquities" (Isa 53:5), that he carried out his greatest act of love. The sins of the human race were in the mystery of God's plan carried to the cross by the God-Man and nailed there (Col 2:14). One Good Friday I heard a black-robed Presbyterian preacher named Elam Davies thunder words that etched themselves into my heart: "If you want to know what God is like," he said, "you must see him in his powerlessness." The powerless God, fastened to a cross of shame, unable even to assuage his own thirst, bearing "our sins in his body on the tree" (1 Pet 2:24), loved us with a love beyond our grasp. Now he invites us, in Thomas' words, to "die with him" (John 11:16). We can offer to God "our selves, our souls and bodies"—selves not fully healed, yet open to God's call.

Third, obey now. Don't wait until you think you're ready. Notice that Hosea didn't wait until he had gotten his personal life in order before he responded to God's call. He said yes to the Lord while the pain was still going on, and in so doing he learned what he needed to learn to share the heart of God with his brothers and sisters. In our world, brokenness is inevitable. We're fallen people, alienated from God, from one another, from ourselves, and from all creation (see Gen 3:14-19). Our world—and our own lives—are broken. The New Testament promises us "an eternal glory that far outweighs" our pain (2 Cor 4:17), but we won't realize that glory fully until we're with the Lord in heaven. In the meantime, we hear God's call and we respond, not because we are ready but simply because he has called.

My friend Pat was in her late 40s when I met her. I never saw her anywhere except on a rented hospital bed in her living room, her body crippled by rheumatoid arthritis. Her leg bones had literally become detached from her hips; her hands were so curled up that she couldn't even push the buttons on her touch-tone phone, let alone hold the instrument. Someone had to feed her, change her clothes, and help her to turn periodically so she wouldn't develop bed sores. Her dreams of a long life to enjoy her children and grandchildren were gone. And yet I must say that God used Pat in a wonderful way. People flocked to her bedside not just to comfort her but to be counseled, encouraged, prayed for. Pat ministered to people from the midst of her brokenness. She didn't call attention to herself or indulge in self-pity. She almost never referred to her physical condition. But somehow, from her brokenness, she touched others.

Jesus, I believe, calls us to that same obedience, by which we may know his grace and his power in our weakness.

---

[1] Frederick Buechner, *Godric* (San Francisco: HarperSanFrancisco, 1980), 168–69.

[2] Henri Nouwen, *The Wounded Healer* (New York: Image, 1979), 83–84.

[3] Ibid., 84.

Questions for Discussion

1.   Hosea perhaps imagined himself as "disqualified," with a dysfunctional family, a broken marriage, and massive inner pain, yet God called him and used him. What "disqualifies" you from God's service or renders you "unfit" to answer his call?

2.   How is God calling you not in spite of your brokenness but rather in the midst of it?

3.   How has God used your times of brokenness as a way of enabling you to be a blessing to others? And how has God used others' brokenness to minister to you?

4.   Many Christians want to wait until "things get back to normal" before responding to God's call. What tempts you to wait? What, on the other hand, encourages you to respond to his call, despite inner or outer chaos?

-12-

GOD'S INTRUSIVE CALL: AMOS

Amos 7:10-15

One morning I found myself driven to pray a radically specific prayer. Four members of my parish were in the final stages of dying of cancer. My emotions were drained, I was physically exhausted, and some days I felt that all I did was counsel dying people or their families. I knew that I was stretched thin, my inner resources depleted. So that morning I closed my office door, sat down at my desk, folded my hands, bowed my head, and prayed out loud. "Lord, I'm sure you know what's happening here," I said. "I'm strung out. I just can't deal with any more dying people. So, Lord, I ask you to see to it that everyone around this church stays healthy. I ask, Lord, that I do not have to handle any more dying people. In Jesus' name. Amen."

No sooner had I raised my head than I heard a knock on my office door. I opened it, and there stood a stranger: an older man, tall but bent, with thin white hair. "You don't know me," he said. "My name is Phil, and I've just been to the doctor. He told me that I have lung cancer, and I've only got a couple of months to live. I don't have a church—haven't been to church in years—but as I drove down the street and saw your church, something told me I should stop in and get some help."

The trouble with God's call is that it often seems to come at the wrong moment: when we are at our most frazzled and feel least able to cope with added stress. "Not now, Lord," we want to say. "I'm not ready!" This may be something of what Amos felt when God "took [him] from tending the flock and said to [him], 'Go, prophesy to my people Israel'" (Amos 7:15). God's call was inconvenient, intrusive, unwelcome. It came at a most awkward time, when Amos had important things to do, obligations to fulfill. So God's call can seem to us as well.

Amos, roughly a contemporary of Hosea, prophesied during the reigns of King Uzziah of Judah in the mid-700s B.C.E. Amos and Hosea (whose tortured story we saw in Chapter 11) came from opposite ends of the promised land—Hosea from the northern kingdom and Amos from Tekoa, a small town about eleven miles from Jerusalem in the southern region of Judah. In the north, it was a time of material prosperity and spiritual poverty. The northern kingdom of Israel enjoyed its greatest territorial expansion under Jeroboam II (2 Kgs 14:23-25). Expansion brought wealth. In the course of his prophecy, Amos mentions "houses adorned with ivory" and "mansions" (Amos 3:15), "beds inlaid with ivory," dinners of "choice lambs and fattened calves," "wine by the bowlful," and "finest lotions" (6:4, 6). People lived comfortably, and there seemed no end to Israel's economic boom.

The cost of this wealth was high in spiritual terms, however. Justice was perverted as law courts served the interests of the wealthy. "You . . . turn justice into bitterness and cast right-eousness to the ground . . . you hate the one who reproves in court and despise him who tells the truth. You trample on the poor and force him to give you grain" (5:7, 10-11). Over and over Amos reports God's indictment of Israel for the oppression of the poor and weak. The rich, he says, had been "skimping the measure, boosting the price and cheating with dishonest scales" (8:5), making wider the gap between the very rich and the very poor. "They sell the righteous for silver, and the needy for a pair of sandals. They trample on the heads of the poor as upon the dust of the ground and deny justice to the oppressed" (2:6-7). Then, as a reminder of Israel's apostasy, Amos tells us that "father and son use the same girl"—presumably a temple prostitute—"and so profane my holy name. They lie down beside every altar on garments taken in pledge" (2:7-8). Israel continued to worship at the "high places" (7:9), the sanctuaries of Canaanite fertility deities, a sign of spiritual unfaithfulness.

The fact that Amos was a foreigner, a citizen of Judah, attacking the sins of Israel, and the fact that he chose to preach at the royal sanctuary in Bethel help to explain the violent reaction to his message.

> Then Amaziah the priest of Bethel [the royal Israelite sanctuary where Amos from Judah prophesied] sent a message to Jeroboam king of Israel: "Amos is raising a conspiracy against you in the very heart of Israel. The land cannot bear all his words. For this is what Amos is saying:
>
>> "'Jeroboam will die by the sword,
>> and Israel will surely go into exile,
>> away from their native land.'"
>
> Then Amaziah said to Amos, "Get out, you seer! Go back to the land of Judah. Earn your bread there and do your prophesying there. Don't prophesy anymore at Bethel, because this is the king's sanctuary and the temple of the kingdom." (7:10-13)

Amaziah assumed that Amos was some kind of "professional prophet" coming in from the outside and overstepping his commission.

But Amos had a very different picture of who he was and how God had called him. "Amos answered Amaziah, 'I was neither a prophet nor a prophet's son, but I was a shepherd, and I also took care of sycamore-fig trees. But the LORD took me from tending the flock and said to me, "Go, prophesy to my people Israel"'" (7:14-15). God's call stretched me, Amos said, and interrupted the peaceful flow of my life.

First, God stretched Amos. This stretching was, to begin with, "professional." Amos possessed a familiar set of skills as a tree-tender and a shepherd. He had no training, on the other hand, in prophetic ministry, and he was careful to point out to Amaziah that he was "neither a prophet nor a prophet's son" (7:14). Amos wanted to distance himself from roving bands of prophets, quasi-professionals called "sons of the prophets" who traveled in groups and hired themselves out to deliver favorable oracles (1 Kgs 20:35; see also 1 Sam 10:10; 2 Kgs 2:3, 5, 7, 15); and so he underscored his work in farming and animal husbandry. Amos stressed that his calling as a prophet moved him away from his "comfort zone," away from the familiar. His prophetic ministry had no connection with his profession, his everyday life, or his ordinary round of duties. As he proclaimed God's word at Bethel, Amos stepped into unknown territory.

Albert Schweitzer was familiar with unknown territory. A musician and a theologian, he became most famous for his work as a physician in Central Africa when God called him to a ministry far removed from his training. So it is with us. Most of us have not been trained to share our faith, to pray for the sick, to serve in a pastoral role with fellow Christians, to lead a small group. Most of us have no special skills that help us apply the Christian faith to our ministry in the workplace. Most of us do not know how to visit prisoners, counsel unwed mothers, or communicate with people outside of our culture. Yet God may call us to any one of these ministries, or to countless others. In many cases, of course, training is available; but the call itself often comes *long before* we have been trained, *long before* we know if we are "suitable" for the job. Like Amos, God calls us to move out of our comfort zones and onto a path where we walk with him by faith.

God stretched Amos in another way too. He stretched Amos politically, putting him into contact with people he otherwise would have avoided. Not only was the task unfamiliar, but so were the people. Amos came from Judah, where the monarch, Uzziah (also called Azariah), "did what was right in the eyes of the LORD" (2 Kgs 15:3; 2 Chr 26:4). He lived in a culture that was not yet as severely apostate as that of the northern kingdom. Kings were still compared to the standard of David, "a man after [God's] own heart" (1 Sam 13:14). But God ordered Amos to cross the border into alien territory to confront the religious and political establishment. To some extent, Israel's culture would be foreign to him. The two kingdoms had been separate for about two hundred years; and although they shared much in common, their development had been parallel, rather than joint, and somewhat divergent. The spiritual, political, economic, and ethical climate in the north would be strange. God required him to deal with people who started with different presuppositions, whose values and attitudes were unlike his, who were quite comfortable worshiping the Lord *and* Baal, who did not share his—and God's—concern for the poor and the weak. Amos would be an alien in an alien culture.

Often God calls us into relationships that cross barriers of race and culture and language, relationships we might not choose if left on our own. He calls us from the world into the church and from the church into the world as we hear Jesus' call to serve him in new and sometimes risky ways. This call is as ancient as the church's first cross-cultural encounter with the Gentiles (see Acts 10) and as contemporary as recent efforts of Baby Boomers to reach out to "Millennials," persons born after 1982. In both cases, God sends us to people who are not like us at all.

God's call impinged on Amos in a second way. *God interrupted Amos.* "The LORD took me from tending the flock and said to me, 'Go'" (Amos 7:15). He was busy; he had a job to do; and in the midst of the job God interrupted him. I've often imagined the dialogue between Amos and the Lord. "Amos, go, prophesy to my people Israel." "But, Lord, the trees need to be watered." "Go." "And they need to be pruned. They're getting all overgrown." "Go." "And the sheep, Lord—they're due for shearing this week." "Go." "But, Lord, you don't understand! I'm a busy man! I've got responsibilities." "Go." I'm working from an assumption here that may simply be my own fantasy—that Amos was a task-oriented person like me, bent on getting the job done. But whatever Amos' inner state when God called him, it's clear that he had tasks hanging over him, that he faced deadlines, that the success of his business depended on his reliability. All of this sounds very familiar as I reflect on my own reaction to God's call. Not now, Lord—I'm not ready!

The New Testament presents us with powerful pictures of the Lord's call as a force that interrupts our lives. Jesus called Peter, Andrew, James, and John while they were involved with their fishing (Mark 1:16-20). His summons to Matthew came as Matthew sat in the tax collector's booth (Matt 9:9). Even more dramatically, Saul—"breathing out murderous threats" (Acts 9:1)—experienced an interruption on the road to Damascus that changed him forever and changed the Church as well.

When people interrupt us with their need, that very need can represent God's call. It is a divine appointment. I surely discovered this with Phil, the man who came to my office door after receiving the diagnosis of terminal lung cancer. In many ways, Phil was an answer to my prayer, though I didn't know it at the time. Jesus came to me in the one who was a stranger and sick, and I was blessed immeasurably in that relationship. Phil turned to Christ at the end of his life, and his conversion became an icon of God's grace as Jesus portrays it in the parable of the workers in the vineyard (Matt 20:1-16). He was a powerful witness to me and to the parish of the Lord's persistent love.

I remember once complaining to a friend that I could never get any work done at the office. Every time I sat down at my desk to do some important paperwork, the phone would ring or somebody would turn up at my door wanting to talk to me about a problem. "How can I ever get anything done with all of these interruptions?" I asked with self-pity. "Ed," my friend told me, "you need to remember that Christians are in the interruption business." How true that is! It is often in the interruptions—the things we haven't counted on or planned for—that the Holy Spirit speaks to us.

This truth is difficult for me —I don't like to set aside a task until it is done. When I imagine God's call in its ideal form, it always comes at a convenient moment, when I am ready to wrap up Task A and turn to Task B. But God rarely calls me or anyone else so neatly. When the Samaritan in Jesus' parable came upon the bloodied victim by the side of the road (Luke 10:30-37), he had to interrupt his journey to care for the man. When Paul exorcised the demon-possessed girl in Philippi (16:16-18), he was on his way to a prayer meeting (Acts 16:16-18). God's call is rarely convenient. It is unlikely to come at a "good" time, when other responsibilities have been dealt with. It interrupts us, intrudes into our daily lives, and demands our attention when we think we have more important things to do.

Like Amos, we too are busy with our trees and our sheep. There are always things to do, commitments to fulfill, tasks that press upon us and deafen us to the Lord's call. So the most dangerous prayer we can pray is the prayer of self-offering: "Lord Jesus, I am yours. I present myself to you, body, soul, and spirit. I make myself available to you and open myself to your call." It's dangerous because this is one prayer the Lord will most surely answer, and in ways that will most surely surprise us.

Questions for Discussion

1.   What represents your "comfort zone," the place where you are confident of your skills and abilities?

2.   How has God challenged you, as he challenged Amos, to move out of a comfort zone and into a place where you lacked competence or training? What was your response? What was the result?

3.   When has God put you into contact with people you might not have chosen—people from a different culture, who speak a different language, whose "Christian vocabulary" differs from yours? How did you react?

4.   God's call rarely comes at a convenient time. How has God interrupted you? Were you able to perceive the interruption as a divine call? If so, how?

-13-

CALLED IN HOLINESS: ISAIAH

Isaiah 6:1-9

For the prophet Isaiah, the word "holy" had special meaning. It wasn't about wondrous spectacles or virtuous people; it wasn't negative, as in "holier than thou." For Isaiah, holiness was about God , whom he called "the Holy One of Israel" (Isa 1:4; 5:19, 24; 10:20; 12:6; et al.). God's holiness and Isaiah's call are inextricably bound together; for in discovering that God is holy, Isaiah saw himself as he really was, "a man of unclean lips" (6:5). He saw the Lord as one "high and exalted" (6:1), and he heard a voice summoning him: "Whom shall I send? And who will go for us?" (6:8).

Isaiah's call is easy to date. "In the year that King Uzziah died I saw the LORD . . ." (Isa 6:1). Uzziah (also called Azariah), who reigned from 792 until 740 B.C.E., receives a "one thumb up, one thumb down" review from the biblical authors. "He did what was right in the eyes of the LORD" (2 Kgs 15:3; 2 Chr 26:4), but on the other hand, he also tolerated pagan practices at the "high places" (2 Kgs 15:4), eventually trying to usurp the priests' prerogatives by offering incense in the temple (2 Chr 26:16). In punishment, God afflicted him with leprosy, a disease that in ancient Israel separated the sufferer from God's people and excluded him from worship (26:19, 21). Isaiah's vision and call, occurring as they did in the temple in the year of Uzziah's death, stand in contrast to the king's pride and presumption.

During Isaiah's prophetic ministry, Judah faced three grave problems. First, the Assyrian empire under Tiglath-Pileser 1 (745-732 B.C.E.) and his successors threatened not only the northern kingdom of Israel, which was destroyed in 722 B.C.E., but Judah as well. Second, the social injustices that Amos had denounced in Israel were now afflicting Judah. "When you spread out your hands in prayer, I will hide my eyes from you; even if you offer many prayers, I will not listen. Your hands are full of blood; wash and make yourselves clean. Take your evil deeds out of my sight! Stop doing wrong, learn to do right! Seek justice, encourage the oppressed. Defend the cause of the fatherless, plead the case of the widow" (Isa 1:15-17). Third, many in Judah followed the lead of their northern brothers and sisters in worshiping other gods. "They are full of superstitions from the East; they practice divination like the Philistines. . . . Their land is full of idols; they bow down to the work of their hands, to what their fingers have made" (2:6, 8). Isaiah, the longest and most complex of the prophetic books, powerfully proclaims God's judgment and God's love and calls his people back to faithfulness. But how did Isaiah's ministry start? It started when he met the Holy God.

Isaiah's call, as reported in the sixth chapter of his book, naturally falls into four movements, each movement blending into the next, illuminating it, moving the action forward to the crescendo of Isaiah's self-offering: "Here am I. Send me!" (Isa 6:8).

First, Isaiah experienced the holiness of God. "In the year that King Uzziah died, I saw the LORD seated on a throne, high and exalted, and the train of his robe filled the temple" (Isa 6:1). Though the vision took place in the temple in Jerusalem, Isaiah glimpsed something more: the heavenly temple, and the worship of the celestial choirs. "Above him were seraphs, each with six wings: With two wings they covered their faces, with two they covered their feet, and with two they were flying. And they were calling to one another: 'Holy, holy, holy is the LORD Almighty; the whole earth is full of his glory.' At the sound of their voices the doorposts and thresholds shook and the temple was filled with smoke" (6:2-4). The seraphs proclaimed that God is "holy, holy,

holy": a threefold emphasis that is meant to brand the holiness of God on our hearts.

When the Bible calls God "holy," it means that he is wholly other, separate beyond imagining. God's holiness takes us far from the comfortable fellowship of the Garden of Eden, where God walked with his creatures in the cool of the day (Gen 3:8). He is "majestic in holiness, awesome in glory" (Exod 15:11); he "lives in unapproachable light" (1 Tim 6:16), further removed from us than we are from single-celled amoebae. "As the heavens are higher than the earth, so are my ways higher than your ways and my thoughts than your thoughts" (Isa 55:9). Even in heaven, the last book of the Bible tells us, we will bow before the Holy God. "In the center, around the throne [of God], were four living creatures. . . . Day and night they never stop saying: 'Holy, holy, holy is the LORD God Almighty, who was, and is, and is to come'" (Rev 4:6, 8). The natural response to the holiness of God is silence and awe and a great trembling.

We encounter God's holiness in many ways. I remember as a college student shortly before my conversion to Christianity sitting in the San Gorgonio mountains of Southern California and looking down into the Coachella Valley. Directly below me was the irrigated green of Palm Springs; beyond, desert that stretched almost into infinity; and then, fifty miles to the southeast, the Salton Sea and more desert, reaching to the horizon. Although I wasn't yet a Christian believer, that view gave me an insight into God's holiness: The God who made the mountains and the endless desert was the same God who had called everything into being, from the macrocreation of galaxies and clusters of galaxies to the microcreation of subatomic particles. I sat cross-legged on a huge boulder and felt something of Jacob's wonder: "How awesome is this place!" (Gen 28:16). But how much more awesome is the Holy God who made it. This should be no surprise, for the Bible tells us that creation points to its Creator. "The heavens declare the glory of God, and the firmament shows his handiwork" (Ps 19:1 BCP). Paul, in fact, tells the Christians in Rome that "since the creation of the world God's invisible qualities—his eternal power and divine nature— have been clearly seen, being understood from what has been made" (Rom 1:20). When we look at creation through the eyes of faith, we see the One who is thrice holy.

For many Christians, worship unveils God's holiness with special intensity. "Worship the LORD in the beauty of holiness; let the whole earth tremble before him" (Ps 96:9 BCP). This has certainly been my experience; no single style of worship triggers an encounter with the Holy God. I've experienced the holiness of God in the reverent offering of centuries-old liturgy, the vestments and the bells and the incense and the music and the candles all reminding my senses that God created us to "declare the praises of him who called [us] out of darkness into his wonderful light" (1 Pet 2:9). I've experienced the holiness of God in the freedom of charismatic worship, song following song, one blending into another, rising in intensity, drawing me out of myself and into the presence of God. I've experienced the holiness of God in the quietness of a Benedictine monastery, where worship is punctuated with long silences where we meet the God who says, "Be still, then, and know that I am God" (Ps 46:11 BCP), the God Elijah met in the "sound of sheer silence" (1 Kgs 19:12 NRSV).

Encountering God's holiness almost inevitably leads to transformation. It was in the setting of worship in the temple that Isaiah met the Holy One, and his life was changed forever. Paul likewise links worship and transformation. "I appeal to you therefore, brothers and sisters, by the mercies of God, to present your bodies as a living sacrifice, holy and acceptable to God, which is your spiritual worship" (Rom 12:1 NRSV). And what is the result of our worship? "Do not be conformed to this world, but be transformed by the renewing of your minds, so that you may discern what is the will of God—what is good and acceptable and perfect" (12:2 NRSV). Worship leads to inner renewal, which opens us to God's call.

Second, Isaiah realized his own unholiness in the presence of the Holy God. After his vision in the temple, Isaiah saw himself as he actually was. "'Woe to me!' I cried. 'I am ruined! For I am a man of unclean lips, and I live among a people of unclean lips, and my eyes have seen the King, the LORD Almighty'" (Isa 6:5). Isaiah knew instinctively that he was in deep trouble. He was broken, sinful, marred—all qualities that stood out starkly in the light of God's holiness. Isaiah's reaction wasn't one of neurotic self-loathing. He was not, like Gideon, tragically afflicted with a poor self-image. No, Isaiah really *was* unclean, and he didn't try to hide the fact. He could have made excuses: "It's true, Lord, I've sinned now and then. But it's not my fault, you see. I was raised in a home with a domineering mother and a father who didn't pay attention to us kids. I never got any affirmation. All I ever heard was criticism, criticism, criticism. Life's done me wrong. I've been trying to get into the prophet business for years, but the Prophets' Union just won't let me in. No wonder I'm angry. I've got a right to be angry. It's not fair!" But Isaiah said none of that. He would have agreed with Paul's citation of Psalm 14 and would not have hesitated to apply that psalm to himself: "There is no one righteous, not even one; there is no one who understands, no one who seeks God. All have turned away, they have together become worthless" (Rom 3:10-12, citing Ps 14:1-3).

When Jesus helped Peter and his companions to haul in a miraculous catch of fish, Peter was horrified. He had caught a glimpse of who Jesus really was, and so "he fell at Jesus' knees and said, 'Go away from me, Lord; I am a sinful man!'" (Luke 5:8). This is how human sin, honestly perceived, responds to the presence of holiness. The 1928 edition of the Episcopal Book of Common Prayer includes a form of general confession with these words: "There is no health in us. But thou, O Lord, have mercy upon us, miserable offenders."[1] The 1979 edition shortens it: "But thou, O Lord, have mercy upon us"—period.[2] No lack of health, no more "miserable offenders"! I am not yearning for the "good old days" of liturgy, but we do shy away from a flat statement of painful and objective truth. We are in fact miserable offenders. Without Christ we are "slaves to sin, which leads to death" (Rom 6:16). We are born with a built-in tendency to rebel against God, and until we have confessed our sin and accepted the forgiveness he so longs to give, we're cut off from him (Col 1:21-22). Isaiah likewise acknowledged his own sinfulness when he cried out, "Woe to me!"

Third, Isaiah was cleansed by the Holy One. "Then one of the seraphs flew to me with a live coal in his hand, which he had taken with tongs from the altar. With it he touched my mouth and said, 'See, this has touched your lips; your guilt is taken away and your sin atoned for'" (Isa 6:6-7). Isaiah could recognize his problem, but he couldn't heal it. God alone could make him clean and fit for his service.

Christians believe that in Christ God has made final and perfect atonement for our sins; the symbols of the Old Testament point to the cross, where the blood of Jesus is poured out for us and the broken body of Jesus bears our sins (2 Cor 5:21; 1 John 1:7). Jesus himself is the burning coal, the cleanser, "the atoning sacrifice for our sins, and not only for ours but also for the sins of the whole world" (1 John 2:2). It's a painful process that involves breaking. To come to God not only confessing our sins but confessing at the same time that we can do nothing about them ourselves means that we are not self-sufficient. We are dependent on God.

Eustace Scrubb made this discovery. In C. S. Lewis's *The Voyage of the Dawn Treader,* young Eustace and his cousins are magically transported to the land of Narnia, where they sail from island to island with King Caspian on a ship called the *Dawn Treader.* Eustace, unfortunately, is a most selfish and disagreeable little boy, and on one island he runs away from his companions and comes upon a dragon's lair. He falls asleep on the enormous pile of gold and jewelry and wakes up transformed—into a dragon! In the process he learns a lesson: He really does miss human companionship; he really does want to become a boy again; he really does want to rejoin the crew. But how? The great lion Aslan comes to him at night and leads him to a well, where he orders Eustace to "undress himself." Eustace manages to scrape off a few layers of dragon skin; but he is still a dragon. Here are Eustace's words:

> Then the lion said—but I don't know if it spoke— "You will have to let me undress you." I was afraid of his claws, I can tell you, but I was pretty nearly desperate now. . . .
>
> The very first tear he made was so deep that I thought it had gone right into my heart. And when he began pulling the skin off, it hurt worse than anything I've ever felt. . . .
>
> Well, he peeled the beastly stuff right off . . . and there it was lying on the grass: only ever so much thicker, and darker, and more knobbly looking than the others had been. And there was I as smooth and soft as a peeled switch and smaller than I had been. Then he caught hold of me—I didn't like that much for I was very tender underneath now that I'd no skin on—and threw me into the water. . . . I'd turned into a boy again."[3]

A "burning coal" hurts because it exposes who we really are. But in being cleansed, we become the persons God has designed us to be.

Fourth, Isaiah was called and commissioned by the Holy One. "Then I heard the voice of the Lord saying, 'Whom shall I send? And who will go for us?' And I said, 'Here am I. Send me!'

He said, 'Go. . .'" (Isa 6:8-9). The order is essential. Isaiah first met the Holy God, and the encounter forced him to face the "real Isaiah," a "man of unclean lips" (6:5). This moment of painful truth put Isaiah in the place where he could be cleansed and forgiven. Then, and only then, was Isaiah ready to hear God's call. "Whom shall I send?" Yes, God had known all along that he would call Isaiah. But there were some necessary steps that Isaiah had to take before he could hear and respond to the summons of God.

And what a summons it was! Not only did Isaiah speak with boldness to the people of his own day, but Christians have read his message with awe for two thousand years. Sprinkled throughout the Book of Isaiah are pointers to the coming Messiah that were fulfilled in Jesus. During Advent we ponder Scriptures that prepare us for the ministry of the forerunner, John the Baptist (Isa 40:1-11). At Christmastime we gaze in wonder at Immanuel (7:14) and remember that "to us a child is born. . . . And he will be called Wonderful Counselor, Mighty God, Everlasting Father, Prince of Peace" (9:6). On Good Friday we are drawn into the mystery of the suffering servant whose wounds make us whole (52:13-53:12). Neither Isaiah nor his followers knew the future. They didn't know that these words, addressing the desperate crises of their own day, would foreshadow the one who would be born "when the time had fully come" (Gal 4:4). But these prophetic words became possible because Isaiah met the Holy One. His heart was broken, and mended, and filled to overflowing—as ours can be as well, if we dare to encounter the holiness of God.

---

[1] Book of Common Prayer (New York: Seabury, 1928), 6.

[2] Book of Common Prayer (New York: Church Hymnal Corp., 1979), 42.

[3] C.S. Lewis, *The Voyage of the Dawn Treader* (New York: Collier, 1952), 90–91.

Questions for Discussion

1.   What brings you most powerfully into an awareness of the Holy God? Worship? The grandeur of nature? People who reflect God's holiness? Silence?

2.   Isaiah's initial response to God's holiness was one of horror. "I am ruined!" How do you react when the holiness of God becomes a reality to you? Does God's holiness bring horror (as it did for Isaiah), joy, awe, or some other emotion?

3.   How do you seek healing or cleansing when your own status as a "miserable sinner" becomes clear to you? Can you think of a time when clarity regarding sin led you to a "burning coal"?

4.   "Whom shall I send?" In what areas of your life do you sense God asking that question today?

-14-

WHEN A CALL BECOMES A BURDEN: JEREMIAH

Jeremiah 1:4-10

"It was really fun at first," Pete said.

Pete was telling me about his ministry in a nearby state penitentiary. For several years he'd been leading a weekly Bible study for inmates, as well as meeting with a few of them for individual counseling sessions. A tax attorney by profession, Pete was knowledgeable about the Bible, articulate about his faith, and a sensitive, caring listener. Many times his counsel had saved me from embarrassing mistakes and guided me as I tried to discern the Lord's will. Now it was Pete who sought counsel.

"I'll never forget the first time I went to the prison," Pete continued. "I was terrified. I mean, tax attorneys don't deal with hard-core criminals—we're pretty insulated. And then that huge set of bars clanged shut behind my back, and the strangest thing happened inside me. All of a sudden, out of the blue, I *knew* I was where God wanted me. I *knew* I was called to that prison. I *knew* there were people I was supposed to help and serve. And there were! Not everyone, you understand—some of the guys come out to the Bible study just to have something to do. But there have always been a few who were really searching, and it was wonderful to see their lives transformed when they committed themselves to Christ."

"I notice you're using the past tense," I said.

"Yes. That's the trouble, you see. It's not that good things aren't happening. It's just that it isn't *exciting* to me anymore. It's getting . . . well, routine. I used to come home floating on air.

Now I come home drained, tired, a little resentful at all the time it takes, wondering why I bother to keep on. Does that mean that it's over?"

Pete's story is the story of every Christian who takes discipleship seriously. Whenever we answer God's call in the affirmative—the initial call to commit our lives to Jesus Christ, or the call to a ministry, a Christian community, or a deeper life of prayer—we experience an initial burst of enthusiasm. But then the enthusiasm begins to fade. It's not that we've stopped believing, or that something has gone wrong. The change is inside, in our hearts. We're not enjoying ourselves anymore, and the call has now become a burden. We begin to wonder: *Am I really supposed to be doing this? Is this actually part of God's plan for me? Or did I hear him incorrectly at the very start?* Our first response to God's call seems to generate its own energy; but in the long haul, after weeks or months or years, we may find our energy depleted, with no replenishment in sight. What are we to do?

Jeremiah found himself in the same boat. God called him to a ministry that lasted more than forty difficult years. There were times when he was discouraged, resentful, and exhausted, and he shows us all this—and more—in his book. But he also allows us to see how, despite the difficulties, God upheld him from the moment of his call. God was faithful to Jeremiah. God is also faithful to us.

God called Jeremiah during a time of national disaster that lasted from "the thirteenth year of the reign of Josiah" (Jer 1:2), roughly 627 B.C.E., through the final destruction of Jerusalem by the Babylonians in 587 B.C.E. to the flight of a small group of Jews to Egypt a few years later. His ministry brought him into constant conflict with secular and spiritual authorities. For Jeremiah, it was just one thing after another: He was threatened with death by the Jerusalem religious establishment (Jer 26:8); a scroll of his writings was set ablaze by the king (36:23); he was arrested on a charge of sedition and thrown into a dungeon (37:11-16); and finally, he was tossed into a cistern full of mud (38:6). At the close of the book, the assassins of the Babylonian-appointed governor, Gedaliah, took Jeremiah and his secretary, Baruch, into unwilling exile in Egypt, despite the prophet's warnings that this action was contrary to the Lord's will (42:13-22). Yet even in Egypt Jeremiah continued to speak God's word as he denounced his fellow Jews for worshiping Egyptian deities. Jeremiah's ministry, from start to finish, was one of discord, isolation, and suffering.

His heart suffered as well. More than any other prophet, Jeremiah paints a painfully honest picture of what went on inside as he struggled to be faithful to God's call. "O my Comforter in sorrow, my heart is faint within me. . . . Oh, that my head were a spring of water and my eyes a fountain of tears! I would weep day and night for the slain of my people" (8:18; 9:1). But through his tears and suffering, Jeremiah never hesitated to challenge God. "You are always righteous, O LORD, when I bring a case before you. Yet I would speak with you about your justice: Why does the way of the wicked prosper? Why do all the faithless live at ease?" (12:1). More than that, Jeremiah revealed his torment as his message was rejected and mocked by the leaders of Judah. "Alas, my mother, that you gave me birth, a man with whom the whole land strives and contends! I have neither lent nor borrowed, yet everyone curses me. . . . Why is my pain unending and my wound grievous and incurable?" (15:10, 18). Eventually the prophet turned his anger toward God himself. "O LORD, you deceived me, and I was deceived; you overpowered me and prevailed. I am ridiculed all day long; everyone mocks me. Whenever I speak, I cry out proclaiming violence and destruction. So the word of the LORD has brought me insult and reproach all day long. But if I say, 'I will not mention him or speak any more in his name,' his word is in my heart like a fire, a fire shut up in my bones. I am weary of holding it in; indeed, I cannot" (20:7-9). Forty years of ministry, lived out in the midst of opposition, took its toll deep in Jeremiah's heart.

"Burnout" may be a modern term, but the concept is as ancient as the Book of Jeremiah. "We use it when people become exhausted with their professions or major life activities. They may find it hard to sleep; they may lose weight or even interest in food; they may have headaches or gastrointestinal disturbances. They may be tired all the time, even after a good night's sleep or a restful vacation. They may be plagued by low-grade, persistent depression or a nagging boredom. They may even act angry or resentful.[1]

We don't know if Jeremiah suffered from the physical symptoms of burnout, but his writing does reveal many of the psychological symptoms. Exhausted by his work and discouraged by a lack of tangible results, he complained bitterly—and in writing. His very name has become associated with a kind of peevish anger. Webster defines "jeremiad" as "a lamenting and denunciatory complaint; a doleful story; a dolorous tirade."[2]

Most Christians aren't beset with the woes that Jeremiah suffered, but still their commitment goes through three inevitable stages. First, there's an initial rush of enthusiasm. The ministry or the commitment carries you forward with its own self-generated excitement. Then comes the second stage, the long haul, when you realize the difficulties you face as you live out your commitment. Things don't come as easily as they used to. Your energy is sapped, your enthusiasm wanes, you may even come to resent the call. Finally, with perseverance, you discover a new and more substantial yielding of your life to Jesus and his purposes, and the fruits of the Spirit (Gal 5:22-23) begin to blossom more fully in your life. It was during the middle stage, the time of struggle and emptiness, that Jeremiah poured out his heart to the Lord. His question—and ours—isn't, How can I avoid burnout? We cannot! Rather, the question is, What does the Lord do to help me survive it and come through with my faith and obedience intact? God answered that question for

Jeremiah by giving him three gifts at the moment of his call. He gives those same gifts to us.

The first gift was the call of God. "The word of the LORD came to me, saying, 'Before I formed you in the womb I knew you, before you were born I set you apart; I appointed you as a prophet to the nations'" (1:4-5). It was important for Jeremiah to know that his call was not an afterthought. On the contrary, God had chosen Jeremiah even before Jeremiah came into existence. God called him, gave him life, made him unique, and wrote him into the divine plan. The psalmist sees this same truth about himself:

> For you yourself created my inmost parts; you knit me together in my mother's womb. I will thank you because I am marvelously made; your works are wonderful, and I know it well. My body was not hidden from you, while I was being made in secret and woven in the depths of the earth. Your eyes beheld my limbs, yet unfinished in the womb; all of them were written in your book; they were fashioned day by day, when as yet there was none of them. (Ps 139:12-15 BCP)

The Bible's teaching is unmistakable. No human being is an accident from God's perspective. Even before we were conceived, God had chosen to give us life. Because he is outside of space and time, the past, present, and future that we call "time" is eternally present to God. Before the creation and the fall, before God's plan to redeem the human race had even begun, God had called Jeremiah—and God called us as well.

We all need to remind ourselves of that fact, especially when burnout threatens to rob our Christian commitment of its joy. When it seems we have nothing left to give, remember that God the Father "chose us in Christ before the foundation of the world to be holy and blameless before him in love. He destined us for adoption as his children through Jesus Christ" (Eph 1:4-5 NRSV). Whatever brought us to faith—an imperceptible spiritual evolution or a sudden and dramatic conversion—God worked in us and through us to draw us to himself. In the bleak times, Jeremiah needed to remember his calling. So do we.

The second gift was the presence of God. Like Moses, Jeremiah objected when he first heard God's call. "'Ah, Sovereign LORD,' I said, 'I do not know how to speak; I am only a child.' But the LORD said to me, 'Do not say, "I am only a child." You must go to everyone I send you to and say whatever I command you. Do not be afraid of them, for I am with you and will rescue you,' declares the LORD" (Jer 1:6-8). God doesn't promise Jeremiah a trouble-free life. "I . . . will rescue you" implies that there will be situations from which Jeremiah would need to be rescued. Some presentations of Christianity today imply—or indeed promise—that when people commit their lives to Jesus Christ their troubles will evaporate: no more health problems, no more crushing bills, no more struggles with personal relationships, no more inner turmoil. Over and over I have seen the damage these distorted presentations of Christianity can do. People come to believe their lives should be free of problems; when troubles arise, as they always do, the result is either a sense of failure and guilt ("What did I do wrong that God didn't heal me?") or a burst of anger ("God let me down!"). But nowhere does the Christian faith guarantee a life without stress or problems. "In this world you will have trouble," Jesus said (John 16:33).

What God promised, however, is that he would be with Jeremiah in the midst of his troubles and that, in the end, God would see him through. Remember, for example, Jeremiah's time in the cistern in Jerusalem. It was a period of terrible desolation for him as he stood in the mud, unable to extricate himself. Eventually God provided a way out. A Cushite named Ebed-Melech approached King Zedekiah and asked for permission to pull Jeremiah from the cistern. Permission was granted, and

Ebed-Melech and his companions "pulled [Jeremiah] up with the ropes and lifted him out of the cistern" (Jer 38:13). The "way out" doesn't erase Jeremiah's terrible sufferings, in this incident and in many others. But it reminds us that just as God was present with Jeremiah, God will be present with us, no matter how bleak our circumstances or how empty our hearts. God's provision of a way out reminds us of God's faithfulness.

The third gift was the word of God. "Then the Lord reached out his hand and touched my mouth and said to me, 'Now, I have put my words in your mouth. See, today I appoint you over nations and kingdoms to uproot and tear down, to destroy and overthrow, to build and to plant'" (1:9-10). This was a very specific promise that God would give Jeremiah precisely the words he would need to deliver the message God wanted to convey. Years later Jeremiah denounced the "false prophets," those who spoke "visions from their own minds, not from the mouth of the Lord" (23:16). In denouncing these prophets, Jeremiah defined what a true prophet really did. "But which of them [the false prophets] has stood in the council of the Lord to see or to hear his word? Who has listened and heard his word? . . . But if they had stood in my council, they would have proclaimed my words to my people and would have turned them from their evil ways and from their evil deeds" (23:18, 22). Reading the passage "backward," gleaning the positive message from the negative word, shows us the true mission of the prophet: to stand in the Lord's council, listen for his word, and faithfully report it. Jeremiah did this for more than forty years. His basic equipment for ministry was God's word.

The Word of God is our basic equipment too. The Christian equivalent of God's promise to Jeremiah is the gift of the Scriptures. The Anglican Articles of Religion say that "Holy Scripture containeth all things necessary to salvation: so that whatsoever is not read therein, nor may be proved thereby, is not to be required of any man, that it should be believed as an article of the Faith."³ We may not have had as dramatic an encounter with the Lord as Jeremiah. God may never have "reached out his hand and touched my mouth" (Jer 1:9). But he has given us the Bible, and in that book he has revealed to us what we need to know about his nature, about his plan to rescue the world from sin and death, and about his purpose for our lives. And so Paul can say, "All scripture is inspired by God and is useful for teaching, for reproof, for correction, and for training in righteousness, so that everyone who belongs to God may be proficient, equipped for every good work" (2 Tim 3:16-17 NRSV). How do we know God? How do we discern his will? How are we made ready for his service? Paul's answer: the Bible.

But there's more. Paul tells us that "we have the mind of Christ" (1 Cor 2:16). God enables us to think the very thoughts of Jesus, to know the heart of the Lord. How? In part, by the indwelling Holy Spirit (John 14:25-26; 1 Cor 2:10-15; 1 John 2:20, 27); and in part, by the regular and systematic reading of Scripture (Rom 15:4; 1 Cor 10:11). All Christians, not just the "professionally religious," need a working knowledge of the Bible to live out their calling.

When the curtain came down on Jeremiah, he was living in exile in Egypt. But I'm awed by Jeremiah's faithfulness. After forty years of ministry—forty years of resistance, ridicule, imprisonment, and the threat of a violent death—he continued to preach the word he'd been given so long before. The gifts of call and presence and word sustained him and empowered him to obey God over the long, long term. They will sustain and empower us too.

---

[1] John A. Sanford, *Ministry Burnout* (New York: Paulist Press, 1982), 1.

[2] *Webster's Third New International Dictionary of the English Language* (Springfield, MA: Merriam, 1969), 1333.

[3] Book of Common Prayer (New York: Seabury, 1928).

Questions for Discussion

1. When have you experienced that deep weariness (or burnout) that robbed you of joy in God's service? What was your initial reaction?

2. In the face of burnout, God reminded Jeremiah, "Before you were born I set you apart." When did you first become aware that God had chosen you to belong to him? Did that awareness dawn slowly or come suddenly?

3. How has God given you a sense of his presence in the midst of sorrow, pain, or failure? What did you do to open yourself to his presence?

4. What part does the Bible play in your own spiritual growth? What are you doing today to "soak in" its message? Are there specific ways the Lord may be challenging you to do more? What are they?

-15-

RESTORING A LOST CALL: ZERUBBABEL

Haggai 1:2-2:9, 23

I caught Hank's eye over the supermarket potato counter. Simultaneously we looked up, spotted each other, and hesitated. I spoke first. "Hank! It's great to see you."

"Yeah. Good to see you, Ed." He paused, his face an odd mixture of embarrassment and defiance. "I guess you're wondering why Margie and I haven't been in church."

I had indeed wondered. Hank and Margie were known as "pillars": active, generous members of the congregation, committed to Christ and the community. Hank was not an educated man; sometimes he had trouble expressing himself clearly. But God had given him a special ministry of prayer, and he became wonderfully articulate when he talked to the Lord. When Hank promised to pray, you *knew* he would pray. I could look around the church on any Sunday and see dozens of people whose lives had been touched by Hank's prayer—including me. Then, five or six months before our potato-counter meeting, Hank and Margie disappeared. They simply stopped showing up at church. Several members of the congregation called them, but Hank and Margie had been vague, almost evasive. Their absence left a spiritual hole in the parish.

"I sure have missed you, Hank," I said, trying to walk that thin line between nosiness and detachment.

"It's this way, see." Hank leaned forward over the counter that separated us. "A few months back Margie and I realized that we hadn't missed a Sunday in years, and so we decided to give ourselves . . . well, sort of a vacation from church, you might say. We figured we'd miss a month or two and then come back. The trouble is, we kind of got used to not going. I'd go down to the pier and fish, and Margie would go to the mall, or we'd both go to the movies. And now, well, our lives are pretty full. We've got lots to do on Sundays, and it's hard to get back in the habit of going to church. I mean, we're not mad or anything, Ed. It's just that we don't seem to have the time anymore."

What happens when Christians lose their sense of call? Most of us do at some point. Our level of commitment starts to slip. It becomes harder and harder to set aside time for prayer or the study of Scripture. We're not as connected to our fellow Christians as we used to be. When the church is looking for volunteers, we hold back. The "fire" burns low. But behind these symptoms lies a deeper problem: We simply don't think about Jesus very much any more. Our lives are busy and full, and Jesus, truth be told, represents one priority among many, squeezed somewhere between the grind of making a living and shopping for groceries and cleaning the house and managing our invest-ment portfolio. We're not resentful of the Lord's demands or overwhelmed by the cost of being a disciple; we're hardly aware that the demands exist. Why does this happen, and what can we do about it? Zerubbabel and his fellow Jews faced their own version of this problem. Through the prophet Haggai, God gave them both a diagnosis of what was wrong and a prescription to restore their lost sense of call.

The Jews carried into exile in Babylon under the mournful eye of Jeremiah were finally permitted to return home when King Cyrus of Persia issued his famous edict in 538 B.C.E. The first wave of returnees left Babylon almost immediately, led by two men, Zerubbabel and Joshua, a priest. Even though Zerubbabel was a descendent of David, the Persian authorities didn't appoint him king—too many nationalistic aspirations were associated with that title. Instead, the Persians named him the governor of Judah and named Joshua the serving high priest and spiritual leader. Within two years the returned exiles began to rebuild the temple destroyed in 587 or 586 B.C.E. The initial steps in reconstruction generated enormous enthusiasm. "All the people gave a great shout of praise to the LORD" (Ezra 3:11).

But the enthusiasm was short lived. By 530 B.C.E. construction had stopped as neighbors began to complain about this sign of a resurgence of Jewish power (Ezra 4:4-5). Even more, the Jews themselves seemed to lose interest. Distracted by their own concerns, they had neither the time nor the resources to invest in restoring the temple. "Thus the work on the house of God in Jerusalem came to a standstill" (Ezra 4:24).

> In the second year of King Darius [520 B.C.E.], on the first day of the sixth month, the word of the LORD came through the prophet Haggai to Zerubbabel son of Shealtiel, governor of Judah, and to Joshua son of Jehozadak, the high priest:
>
> This is what the LORD Almighty says: "These people say, 'The time has not yet come for the LORD's house to be built.'"
>
> Then the word of the LORD came through the prophet Haggai: "Is it time for you yourselves to be living in your paneled houses, while this house remains a ruin?" (Hag 1:1-4)

The Jews had undergone a shift in priorities. When they arrived in Jerusalem in 538 B.C.E., the first thing they did was to plan for the rebuilding of the temple. They procured building materials, organized laborers, and laid the foundation. But eventually other concerns intervened. People had houses to build, a living to make, families to raise. They didn't reject God's call to rebuild the temple; they simply lost sight of it. The pressing issues of daily living overrode the less "practical" set of priorities associated with the temple. For many of Jerusalem's citizens, the partially built temple simply became part of the landscape, with no greater significance than any other abandoned construction site.

Zerubbabel, Joshua, and the Jews didn't struggle with the burnout described in Jeremiah's memoirs. While burnout is the ongoing depletion of spiritual and emotional energy with no corresponding refueling, the temple-builders were dealing with *fade-out,* which sets in when the tyranny of immediate concerns places God's call on the back burner. They didn't reject the call; they just forgot about it.

There's much in our lives to distract us too. Good things— worthwhile and sometimes necessary things—can take over our hearts and minds so that we no longer remember who we are in Christ and what he has called us to do. Paying the bills, getting ahead in our careers, taking care of the house and the yard, spending time with the children, serving on church commit- tees—all of these are part of life and may represent elements of our divine calling. But the sum total of these pressing demands can cause our awareness of God's call to fade out of our lives.

The Last Battle, the final volume of C. S. Lewis' Narnia series, describes the Narnian equivalent of the end of the age. All of the children who had traveled from our world to Narnia appear for the ultimate conflict between Aslan and the forces of evil. Peter, Edmund, Lucy, Jill, Eustace, Polly—they are all there, except one. King Tirian of Narnia counts the children and then turns to Peter.

> "Sir," said Tirian, when he had greeted all these. "If I have read the chronicle aright, there should be another. Has not your Majesty two sisters? Where is Queen Susan?"
>
> "My sister Susan," answered Peter shortly and gravely, "is no longer a friend of Narnia."
>
> "Yes," said Eustace, "and whenever you've tried to get her to come and talk about Narnia or do anything

> about Narnia, she says, 'What wonderful memories you have! Fancy your still thinking about all those funny games we used to play when we were children.'"
>
> "Oh Susan!" said Jill. "She's interested in nothing nowadays except nylons and lipstick and invitations. She always was a jolly sight too keen on being grown-up."[1]

Susan, sadly, suffers from fade-out. So do we. We live in a "recreational culture," one in which we always have something to do. When we're not working or going to school or doing chores, we can attend sports events, drive to a mountain cabin, take a trip in the RV, go to the movies, rent a DVD, or surf the web. For many of us, the Christian Church—in fact, the Christian life as a whole—has become a "recreational option." It happened to Hank and Margie. It happened to Zerubbabel. In subtle ways, it happens to all of us.

But God renewed Zerubbabel's call and brought him back. God's message to the Jews through Haggai was directed primarily at the two leaders, Zerubbabel and Joshua, but the Lord's final word was pointed at Zerubbabel alone (Hag 2:23). As a descendant of King David, Zerubbabel had a special place in God's plan. The Lord had three words for Zerubbabel and his companions concerning their lost call.

First, remember the terms of my call to you. "Give careful thought to your ways. Go up into the mountains and bring down timber and build the house, so that I may take pleasure in it and be honored" (1:7-8). The Jews had been diverted from their first priority in favor of more immediate and pressing concerns. You must recommit yourselves, God told them, to rebuilding this symbol of my presence in your midst. God went on to remind them that their disobedience had consequences.

> "Give careful thought to your ways. You have planted

much, but have harvested little. You eat, but never have enough. You drink, but never have your fill. You put on clothes, but are not warm. You earn wages, only to put them in a purse with holes in it. . . .

"I called for a drought on the fields and the mountains, on the grain, the new wine, the oil and whatever the ground produces, on men and cattle, and on the labor of your hands." (1:5-6, 11)

The Lord urged Zerubbabel and the Jews to give "careful thought" both to their call and to the unavoidable results of disobedience.

Fade-out has serious consequences. When our priorities change, the lordship of Jesus Christ may move from the center of our lives to the periphery, one interest among many. But the transition is slow, subtle, and we're often not aware that it's even happening.

So we need to be reminded, often and loudly, of what it means to commit our lives to Jesus Christ and respond to his call. In the Old Testament, God's people sometimes renew their covenant with the Lord (for example, in Joshua 24), not so much to remind God of his responsibilities as to remind them of theirs! We require something similar—a way of helping us keep our commitment to Jesus on the front burner of our hearts. In the Diocese of Northern Indiana, for example, we have developed a set of four "core values" intended to give shape to our vision of mission and ministry. They are

a passion for the Gospel of Jesus Christ
a heart for the lost
a willingness to do whatever it takes
a commitment to one another

These "core values" turn up everywhere: on the front page of every edition of the diocesan newspaper, in parish newsletters, on prayer cards distributed to all communicants of the diocese, in the mission statements of many congregations, in sermons and workshops and teachings. You can't be a member of any parish in the diocese for very long and escape the "core values." They're our equivalent of the stone that Joshua set up to remind the Israelites of their covenant with the Lord (Josh 24:25-27). Zerubbabel and his companions had forgotten the terms of their call, and the result was disaster, spiritually and materially. As communities and individuals, we benefit from such reminders.

God had a second word for Zerubbabel, Joshua, and the Jews of Jerusalem: *Remember who I am.* The people had become so wrapped up in their daily concerns that they had lost their awe of the God who had rescued his people—twice!—from bondage. Focus on me, God said in effect, and you will recover your call. Remember my presence among you. "Then Haggai, the LORD's messenger, gave this message of the LORD to the people: 'I am with you,' declares the LORD. . . . 'Be strong, all you people of the land,' declares the LORD, 'and work. For I am with you'" (Hag 1:13; 2:4). Even when his people ignored him, God would be present in their midst.

God's presence is inextricably bound up with the covenant he had established with his people. "This is what I covenanted with you when you came out of Egypt. And my Spirit remains among you. Do not fear" (Hag 2:5). The word "covenant" would trigger all sorts of memories in the minds of the Jews: God's covenant with Abraham, his mighty deeds when he delivered the Israelites from Egypt, the covenant at Mount Sinai and the giving of the law. The whole package of memories would remind the Jews that their God was a faithful God, "the compassionate and gracious God, slow to anger, abounding in love and faithfulness, maintaining love to thousands, and forgiving wickedness, rebellion and sin" (Exod 34:6-7). Remember, God said, that I love you so much that I have bound myself to you by solemn covenant. Christians too have been bound to God by covenant: the new covenant prophesied by Jeremiah (Jer 31:31-34), mediated by Jesus (Heb 9:15), and commemorated in the Eucharist (1 Cor 11:25). Every time we gather at the Lord's Table to celebrate the Eucharist, we renew our participation in the covenant that Jesus inaugurated in his death and resurrection. Our God is a covenant God; his nature is to reach out to us and draw us to himself—something Zerubbabel and his companions needed to recall. I am faithful to you, the Lord said. Now you must respond to me in obedience, and my Spirit will empower you.

God had a third and final word directed specifically to Zerubbabel: *Remember who you are.* "'On that day,' declares the LORD Almighty, 'I will take you, my servant Zerubbabel son of Shealtiel,' declares the LORD, 'and I will make you like my signet ring, for I have chosen you,' declares the LORD Almighty" (Hag 2:23). An ancient king wore a signet ring so that he could stamp documents to prove their authenticity. The ring was almost a part of him, a reminder of his royal status and power. Years earlier, Zerubbabel's grandfather Jehoiachin had also been compared to a signet ring, with a dreadful result. "'As surely as I live,' declares the LORD, 'even if you, Jehoiachin son of Jehoiakim king of Judah, were a signet ring on my right hand, I would still pull you off'" (Jer 22:24), so rebellious had Judah become. But now Jehoiachin's grandson would take his rightful place as the Lord's signet ring, close to God's heart and the object of his love. When you suffer from fade-out, God told Zerubbabel, remember who you are in my sight. Remember that I have chosen you.

The image of the signet ring has special meaning for me. I often wear an episcopal signet ring, a reminder of my call as Bishop of Northern Indiana. On the ring is inscribed the seal of the diocese: a miter on top, a lighthouse in the center, Greek words from John's Gospel (1:4, "the light of all people") at the bottom. The ring reminds me that I belong to God and that, by his grace and beyond all deserving, I have been inscribed on his heart. Indeed, so have we all. Marked as his own in baptism, sealed (literally, stamped!) by his Spirit, we are Christ's own forever.

God didn't choose Zerubbabel randomly. He was part of a much wider plan, God's ultimate rescue mission: the life, death, and resurrection of Jesus Christ. Both Matthew (1:12-13) and Luke (3:27) place Zerubbabel among the ancestors of the Savior. He fulfilled a mission of infinitely greater importance than the building of the new temple, and his preciousness to the Lord was set in bold type. But Zerubbabel didn't know the future. He only knew God's command for the present moment: Build my house. Remember who you are. Remember how much I love you and how precious you are in my sight. Remember that you are as close to me as the ring on a king's finger.

When our spiritual vision begins to fade and our sense of call evaporates with it, we need to take concrete steps to "confirm [our] call and election" (2 Pet 1:10 NRSV). God's word to Zerubbabel and his companions sets out the process: Remember the terms of your call; remember who I am; remember who you are. It was this final word that eventually touched Hank and Margie. For several months after our potato-counter meeting, they continued to stay away; but their friends in the body of Christ were persistent. You are loved, you are loved, you are loved, their friends kept on saying. In the end, Hank and Margie came to believe that they were indeed loved, not only by their fellow Christians but by Jesus himself. Remembering, finally, who they were, they came home.

---

[1] C.S.Lewis, *The Last Battle* (New York: Collier, 1956), 134–35.

Questions for Discussion

1.   Can you think of a time when your commitment to Christ or to Christian ministry seemed to "fade out"? Did you realize that it was happening? What did you do? Is there a way in which you're experiencing fade-out today?

2.   How can you "re-call" your calling? What Scripture verses or songs or events or persons can remind you of the Lord's first touch in your life?

3.   How do you most powerfully experience God's presence? What "triggers" can reconnect you with the indwelling presence of the Lord?

4.   God describes Zerubbabel as his "signet ring," so close did God hold him to his heart. How would God describe you? Is his love for you a living reality? If not, how can God's love become real to you?

-16-

CALLED BY CIRCUMSTANCES: ESTHER

Esther 4:1-5:2

Rokuemon Hasekura couldn't rid his mind of the grue-some image of Christ crucified. Shusaku Endo tells his story in *The Samurai*, a novelist's meditation on martyrdom-by-accident. Rokuemon, a seventeenth-century Japanese warrior and a loyal subject of the emperor, agrees to accompany a diplomatic entourage to Mexico (and ultimately to Rome) to secure trade privileges for Japan. The long journey exposes Rokuemon for the first time to the Christian faith. Rokuemon is confused by what he sees: massive church buildings, Christian civilization at its most impressive . . . and yet, everywhere, a symbol of defeat: Jesus on the cross. "Why do they worship him?" Rokuemon asks.[1] For the sake of the mission, Rokuemon and his companions agree to be baptized as Christians. "When the three [Japanese] bent their heads, the bishop took the silver pitcher from the priest and sprinkled their foreheads with water. . . . A mere formality to the envoys, an irrevocable sacrament to the Church."[2]

This "mere formality" leads to Rokuemon's death. The trade mission fails and the envoys return in disgrace to Japan, where they discover that the political climate has changed. Christians are no longer tolerated; they are persecuted unto death. Rokuemon, the accidental Christian, numbers among them. He is arrested, condemned, executed. Before his death, his mind returns to the emaciated man he had seen over and over in Mexico and Europe, and he remembers a poem a Japanese Christian (a genuine Christian!) had shared with him:

"He is always beside us.

He listens to our agony and our grief.
He weeps with us.
And He says to us,
'Blessed are they who weep in this life, for
in the kingdom of heaven they shall smile.'

"He" was that man with the drooping head, that man
as scrawny as a pin, that man whose arms stretched
lifelessly out, nailed to a cross. Again the samurai
closed his eyes and pictured the man who had peered
down at him each night from the walls of his rooms
in Nueva España and España. For some reason he did
not feel the same contempt for him he had felt before."[3]

Circumstances seemed to maneuver Rokuemon Hasekura
into the kingdom of God. Were they random events? Or the
hand of God himself?

We often find ourselves asking that same question. An
employer offers you a new job, a promotion, a move to another
part of the country. Is this the call of God? The Sunday school
superintendent asks you to teach the junior high class. Is this the
call of God? An aged aunt who has always been hostile to the
Christian faith lies dying in a hospital, and you wonder if you
should try one last time to present the Gospel to her. Is this the
call of God? How do we know when the circumstances of our
lives represent God's summons? Not every job offer, not every
invitation to ministry, not every need that crosses our path is
necessarily a personal summons from the Lord of the universe.
But it may be, and there, precisely, is our problem. How can we
recognize the hand of God in the apparently random events of
our day-to-day lives?

A young woman named Esther faced these questions, and
her answer determined not only her own destiny but that of her
people. In the fifth century B.C.E., the Persian Empire dominated

the entire Middle East, from modern-day Iran and Iraq, through Turkey, down the coast of Syria, Lebanon, and Palestine, and into Egypt. God's people the Jews were scattered throughout this enormous swath of territory. Many had returned to their homeland following the edict of Cyrus in 538 B.C.E., but others stayed and prospered in the land of their exile. Among them was Mordecai, who lived in Susa, the capital of Persia (Est 2:5-6). When King Xerxes sought a new queen, he chose Mordecai's cousin Hadassah (her Persian name was Esther) over thousands of beautiful candidates. "The king was attracted to Esther more than to any of the other women, and she won his favor and approval more than any of the other virgins. So he set a royal crown on her head and made her queen" (2:17). At Mordecai's direction, Esther kept secret her Jewish identity (2:10).

Quickly a crisis erupted. A Persian official named Haman resented Mordecai's lack of deference. "All the royal officials at the king's gate knelt down and paid honor to Haman, for the king had commanded this concerning him. But Mordecai would not kneel down or pay him honor" (3:2). So Haman decided to destroy not only Mordecai but "all Mordecai's people, the Jews, throughout the whole kingdom of Xerxes" (3:6). Cleverly, Haman presented to Xerxes a series of distortions about the Jews—they were "different," they disobeyed the king's laws (3:8)—as anti-Semites have done ever after. The king, perhaps only half-aware of the extent of Haman's designs, gave his counselor free reign. "Do with the people as you please," Xerxes said; and an edict was issued with orders to "kill and annihilate all the Jews—young and old, women and little children—on a single day" (3:11, 13).

That left Esther as the only Jew with direct access to the king. She alone had the potential of stopping a holocaust. Was this God's call to her? Her story reveals something of the answer.

First, Esther found herself caught in circumstances beyond her control. Mordecai, through an intermediary, informed Esther of the king's edict and "urge[d] her to go into the king's presence to beg for mercy and plead with him for her people" (4:8). Life— or perhaps God himself—had put Esther in an incredibly awkward position. Persian law forbade anyone, even the queen, to approach the king unbidden. "For any man or woman who approaches the king in the inner court without being summoned," Esther told Mordecai, "the king has but one law: that he be put to death. The only exception to this is for the king to extend the gold scepter to him and spare his life" (4:11). And so Esther was trapped. To do nothing meant death for her people. To do something potentially meant death for herself and the end of the Jews' last hope. Yet there was no one else to act, no "second string," no hero or heroine waiting in the wings should Esther decline Mordecai's plea.

Often, it seems, life—or perhaps God himself—maneuvers us into just such a place. Some years ago, for example, an elderly aunt of mine did in fact lie dying in a hospital. Aunt Harriet and I had never gotten along. For as long as I had known her, she was a practicing occultist. She gave psychic readings, dabbled in astrology, told fortunes with cards and tea leaves, claimed that she had tried all the "-isms" (in which she included the Christian faith) and found them spiritually unsatisfying. To make matters worse, whenever we were together at family gatherings, she insisted on telling me about her occult practices; and she was so deaf that even if I tried to reply, she couldn't hear me. I avoided her whenever I could. Then, quite suddenly, doctors diagnosed pancreatic cancer and gave Aunt Harriet only days to live. At first, to be honest, I shrugged and went about my business. But gradually, over a period of two or three days, I began to realize that if anyone was going to present the gospel to Aunt Harriet, it was I. There was simply no one else.

I argued with God about this. "Don't you realize," I asked him, "that Aunt Harriet is a lost cause? She hardened her heart against you so long ago that nothing can break through." I heard no answer, just a profound silence—and the continuing, nagging sense that there was nobody but I who could do this thing. Finally, reluctantly, I drove to Oceanside, a community a few miles north of San Diego, and found Aunt Harriet in the intensive care unit. She was lucid but weak and of course virtually deaf. After attempting a few pleasantries, I put my mouth near her ear and shouted, "Aunt Harriet, do you want to invite Jesus into your heart?" My voice echoed around the room. People all over the intensive care unit, from nurses to aides to patients, looked up in surprise. This was not going to be a private conversation! To my surprise, Harriet said, "Yes." And so she prayed with me that day, a prayer of surrender to Jesus who had loved her from all eternity. A few days later she died, a sister in Christ.

Second, then, Mordecai asked a question that enabled Esther to see meaning behind the circumstances. When Esther looked at the danger she faced in approaching the king, she wavered—this, after all, was dangerous business. So Mordecai challenged her: "Do not think that because you are in the king's house you alone of all the Jews will escape. For if you remain silent at this time, relief and deliverance for the Jews will arise from another place, but you and your father's family will perish" (4:13-14). Mordecai reminded Esther that silence provided no ultimate safety; and then he asked, "And who knows but that you have come to royal position for such a time as this?" (4:14).

The Book of Esther is the only document in the Bible that doesn't mention the name of God, yet God's providential care pervades the book from start to finish, especially in Mordecai's question. Mordecai asked Esther to look at her circumstances through God's eyes. It wasn't that God caused Haman to seek destruction of the Jews. It was simply that God, knowing the peril his people faced, put a young Jewish girl in a strategic place at a strategic moment—a young Jewish girl who needed help discerning the hand of God.

I needed such help in discernment too, long ago. It was like this: For many years, I had treated the word "Bakersfield" as a joke. This midsized central California city was by reputation hot, dusty, and cultural light years away from the glitter of Southern California and the Bay Area. "If I don't mind my p's and q's," I would often say in sermons, "the Bishop's going to get mad and send me to . . . [long pause, for effect] . . . Bakersfield." God, apparently, listens to sermons, and so in 1986 the vestry of All Saints Episcopal Church in Bakersfield invited me to come and be its new rector. By then, of course, I had discovered that Bakersfield's reputation was undeserved. But the vestry's invitation set off something of a crisis in me. I found myself asking questions about my "career" (what a ghastly and inappropriate word for ministry!) and my future. Was I banishing myself to the ecclesiastical hinterland? Would I disappear into the vast spaces of the San Joaquin Valley, never to be heard from again? At a distance of more than fifteen years, the questions sound bizarre and faithless. But at the time, they haunted me. Finally, unable to come to a decision, I went on retreat to a mountain cabin, joined by a long-time friend and fellow priest, Brian. "This is a step backward," I kept on saying to Brian. "What does this mean for my 'career track'?" Brian said, "Maybe the point isn't 'career-track.' Could the issue instead be 'kingdom-track'?" That question caused something to "click" in my heart and mind, and I knew—I simply knew—that God had called me to Bakersfield. I have never regretted my decision.

A well-placed question can often illuminate the meaning of an event, helping us to see it from a divine perspective.

Third, Esther made a choice. I imagine a long pause between 4:14 and 4:15, as Esther pondered her call and the possible outcomes of her decision. Finally, agonizingly, she acted. "Then Esther sent this reply to Mordecai: 'Go, gather together all the Jews who are in Susa, and fast for me. Do not eat or drink for three days, night or day. I and my maids will fast as you do. When this is done, I will go to the king, even though it is against the law.

And if I perish, I perish'" (4:15-16). Conventional wisdom and a healthy sense of self-preservation indicated that she should leave well enough alone. The tide of custom, history, and political power threatened to overwhelm any move she might make. Common sense said: Let my fellow Jews take care of themselves; I'll stay here, safe and protected, a hidden Jew in Xerxes' harem. All of that, in some form, must have run through Esther's mind. But still she made the dangerous decision to obey God's call.

Don't underestimate the weight of this moment. It was not only the fate of the Jews that hung in midair, awaiting Esther's decision. It was our fate as well. God's plan of redemption runs in a line from the call of Abraham through the formation of the Israelite nation at the Red Sea and Sinai, on to the kingship of David and his descendants, through the exile in Babylon and return, down to the incarnation, life, death, and resurrection of Jesus Christ. The Jewish people stand at the center of God's plan. Jesus comes to us as a descendant of the chosen people, son of Abraham, heir of David, the longed-for Messiah. Had Esther refused God's call—a possibility well within her range of options—had Haman's plan succeeded, there would have been no Christmas, no Good Friday, no Easter, no Pentecost. We shouldn't be surprised that Jews to this day continue to celebrate Esther's courage on the feast of Purim (9:26-28). Perhaps Christians ought to do the same. Our salvation owes its fulfillment in part to the decision of one terrified and lonely Jewish girl.

Indeed, this moment finds its parallel in a house in Nazareth nearly five centuries later. Another terrified and lonely Jewish girl heard words that demanded decision. "Do not be afraid, Mary, you have found favor with God. You will be with child and give birth to a son, and you are to give him the name Jesus" (Luke 1:30-31). As in Esther's case, I imagine a long pause, the angels in heaven "holding their breath" as they waited to see what this girl would do. Like Esther, Mary responded—finally, agonizingly: "I am the Lord's servant. . . . May it be to me as you have said" (Luke 1:38). Because Mary said yes to God's call, we can read: "The Word became flesh and made his dwelling among us. We have seen his glory, the glory of the One and Only, who came from the Father, full of grace and truth" (John 1:14).

There still, of course, remained the moment of action for Esther. "On the third day Esther put on her royal robes and stood in the inner court of the palace, in front of the king's hall. The king was sitting on his royal throne in the hall, facing the entrance. When he saw Queen Esther standing in the court, he was pleased with her and held out to her the gold scepter that was in his hand. So Esther approached and touched the tip of the scepter" (Est 5:1-2). The king overrode his own law that no one could approach him unbidden. This act of royal favor led in rapid succession to two banquets (5:5-8; 7:1-2), honors for Mordecai (6:1-14), death for Haman (7:9-10), triumph for the Jews (8:1-9:17), and great rejoicing (9:18-32). The events that bring the Book of Esther to a climax were set in motion by one act of obedience, one response to circumstances, one "yes" in the heart of a young woman whose instincts told her to run and hide.

In like manner, the small Protestant village of Le Chambon in southern France produced one of World War II's greatest stories of courage. There, under the nose of Nazi occupation forces and Vichy spies, villagers organized to hide thousands of Jews destined for extermination in the death camps. Under the leadership of Pastor Andre Trocme, ordinary Christians risked their lives to save Jews. At one point, an official of the Reformed Church of France tried to convince Trocme to cease this dangerous activity. "What you are doing is endangering the very existence not only of this village but of the Protestant church of France! You must stop helping them." Trocme responded, "If we stop, many of them will starve to death, or die of exposure, or be deported and killed. We cannot stop." "You must stop," the official said. "The marshall will take care of them. He will see to it that they are not hurt." But Pastor Trocme simply said, "No."[4]

Philip Hallie, author and chronicler of the events of Le Chambon, later tried to make sense of the events of Le Chambon. "One way of judging the Chambonnais is their way—with a shrug of the shoulders and the question: 'Well, where else could they go? I had to take them in.'"[5] That simple question somehow illuminated the meaning of the devastating circumstances and revealed the call of God.

None of us can imagine ourselves making the sort of life-and-death decisions that faced Esther, Mary, and the people of Le Chambon. Most of our choices are infinitely smaller. They have to do with taking this or that job, buying this or that house, spending our money on this or that priority, using our time for this or that project, saying yes or no to this or that "inner prompting." The circumstances that confront us seem insignificant against the vast scheme of God's plan of redemption. Yet in our lives these moments form the building blocks of discipleship, when Jesus beckons us to follow him, when he encourages us to seek his voice amid the tumble of events that confront us every day.

Circumstances alone don't compel obedience. They provide, at best, an invitation. But they may bring the events in which our faith is tested. Like Esther, our first reaction is perhaps to rear back in fear. Can I be the only one? Isn't there someone else? Someone better positioned, better trained, more equipped to face the challenge? And like Esther, we may discover that we are the one; there is no one else. We may find that God has called us from all eternity for just this moment.

---

[1] Shusako Endo, *The Samurai* (New York: New Dimensions, 1982), 159.

[2] Ibid., 175.

[3] Ibid., 242.

[4] Philip Hallie, *Lest Innocent Blood Be Shed* (New York: Harper Torchbooks, 1979), 143.

[5] Ibid., 286.

Questions for Discussion

1.   Esther seemed trapped by circumstances. There was no one but her to save the Jews. Can you think of a time when life or God seemed to maneuver you into a decision? What did you do?

2.   How can we recognize when a circumstance reveals the call of God? What are the signs for you that a circumstance is not simply chance but a divine directive?

3.   How have others helped you to see God's hand in the events of your life? Has anyone been a "Mordecai" for you? How did you react to his or her guidance?

4.   What are the circumstances today that may be unveiling God's call to you? Is God speaking subtly through those circumstances, or powerfully and unmistakably? How will you make a decision about your response?